FRANZ SCHUBERT

A BIOGRAPHY

SCHUBERT AT THE PIANO, Gustav Klimt, 1899. Detail.

FRANZ SCHUBERT

A BIOGRAPHY BY

HENRY FROST

WITH AN INTRODUCTION BY

WILLIAM HADOW

A DISTANT MIRROR

Publisher · Bendigo

Trio in E♭ major, D929.

Originally published in 1892
by Sampson, Low, Marston & Co., London.

This edition published in 2017 by

A DISTANT MIRROR

WEB www.adistantmirror.press

EMAIL hello@adistantmirror.press

Edited and revised by David Major.
dmajor@adistantmirror.press

ISBN-13: 978-1482379990

ISBN-10: 1482379996

Design: D. Major

Printed and bound in the USA.

CONTENTS

1875 oil painting by Wilhelm August Rieder.

1

INTRODUCTION*

FRANZ PETER SCHUBERT was born on the 31st of January 1797, in the Himmelpfortgrund, a small suburb of Vienna. His father, Franz, son of a Moravian peasant, was a parish schoolmaster; his mother, Elizabeth Fitz, had before her marriage been cook for a Viennese family. Of their fourteen children nine died in infancy; the others were Ignaz (b.1784), Ferdinand (b.1794), Karl (b.1796), Franz and a daughter Theresia (b.1801). The father, a man of worth and integrity, possessed some reputation as a teacher, and his school, in the Lichtenthal, was well attended. He was also a fair amateur musician, and transmitted his own measure of skill to his two elder sons, Ignaz and Ferdinand.

At the age of five Schubert began to receive regular instruction from his father. At six he entered the Lichtenthal school where he spent some of the happiest years of his life. About the same time his musical education began. His father taught him the rudiments of the violin, his brother Ignaz taught him the rudiments of the piano.

At seven, having outgrown his teachers, he was placed in the charge of Michael Holzer, the Kapellmeister of the Lichtenthal Church. Holzer's lessons seem to have consisted mainly in expressions of admiration, and the boy gained more from a friendly joiner's apprentice, who would take him to a

---

* This introduction was originally the entry for Schubert in the 1911 edition of the *Encyclopaedia Britannica*.

The house in which Schubert was born, today Nussdorfer Strasse 54, in the 9th district of Vienna.

neighbouring piano warehouse and give him the opportunity of practising on a better instrument than the poor home could afford. The unsatisfactory character of this early training was the more serious because at that time, a composer had little chance of success unless he could appeal to the public as a performer, and for this Schubert's meagre early education was never sufficient.

In October 1808 he was received as a scholar at the Convict, which, under Salieri's direction, had become the chief music school of Vienna, and which had the special responsibility of training the choristers for the Court Chapel. Here he remained

The Convict, the leading music school in Vienna.

until nearly seventeen, profiting little by the direct instruction, which was almost as careless as that given to Haydn at St Stephen's, but he gained much from the practices of the school orchestra, and by association with congenial comrades. Many of the most devoted friends of his later life were among his schoolfellows: Spaun and Stadler and Holzapfel, and a score of others who helped him out of their slender pocket money, bought him music paper which he could not buy for himself, and gave him loyal support and encouragement.

It was at the Convict, too, that he first made acquaintance with the overtures and symphonies of Mozart — there is as yet no mention of Beethoven — and between them and lighter pieces, and occasional visits to the opera, he began to lay for himself some foundation of musical knowledge.

Meanwhile his genius was already showing itself in composition. A piano fantasia, 32 close-written pages, is dated April 8 to May 1, 1810: then followed, in 1811, three long vocal pieces written to a plan which Zumsteeg had popularized,

Franz Schubert as a youth

together with a 'quintet overture,' a string quartet, a second piano fantasia and a number of songs.

His effort in chamber music is noticeable, since we learn that at the time a regular 'quartet party' was established at his home on Sundays and holidays, in which his two brothers played the violin, his father the cello, and Franz himself the viola. It was the first germ of that amateur orchestra for which, in later years, many of his compositions were written.

During the remainder of his stay at the Convict he wrote a good deal more chamber music, several songs, some miscellaneous pieces for the piano and, among his more ambitious efforts, a *Kyrie* and *Salve Regina*, an octet for wind instruments — said to commemorate the death of his mother, which took place in 1812 — a cantata, words and music for his father's name-day in 1813, and the closing work of his school life, his first symphony.

At the end of 1813 he left the Convict, and to avoid military service, entered his father's school as a teacher of the lowest class. For over two years he endured the drudgery of the work, which, we are told, he performed with indifferent success.

There were, however, other interests to compensate. He took private lessons from Salieri, who annoyed him with accusations of plagiarism from Haydn and Mozart, but who did more for his training than any of his other teachers; he formed a close friendship with a family named Grob, whose daughter Therese was an excellent singer and a good friend. He occupied every moment of leisure with rapid and voluminous composition.

His first opera — *Des Teufels Lustschloss* — and his first mass, in F, were both written in 1814, and to the same year belong three string quartets, many smaller instrumental pieces, the first movement of the Symphony in B♭ and seventeen songs, which include such masterpieces as *Der Taucher* and *Gretchen am Spinnrade*.

But even this activity is far outpaced by that of the *annus mirabilis* 1815. In this year, despite his schoolwork, his lessons with Salieri and the many distractions of Viennese life, he produced an amount of music the record of which is almost incredible. The Symphony in B♭ was finished, and a third, in D major, added soon afterwards. Of church music there appeared two masses, in G and B♭, the former written within six days, a new *Dona nobis* for the Mass in F, a *Stabat Mater* and a *Salve Regina*. Opera was represented by no less than five works, of which three were completed — *Der Vierjährige Posten*, *Fernando* and *Claudine von Villabella* — and two, *Adrast* and *Die beiden Freunde von Salamanca*, apparently left unfinished.

Besides these the list includes a string quartet in G minor, four sonatas and several smaller compositions for piano, and, by way of climax, 146 songs, some of which are of considerable length, and of which eight are dated Oct. 15, and seven Oct. 19.

"Here," we may say with Dryden, "is God's plenty." Music

has always been the most generous of the arts, but it has never, before or since, poured out its treasure with so lavish a hand.

In the winter of 1814-15, Schubert met the poet Mayrhofer: an acquaintance which, according to his usual habit, soon ripened into a warm and intimate friendship. They were singularly unlike in temperament: Schubert was frank, open and sunny, with brief fits of depression, and sudden outbursts of boisterous high spirits; Mayrhofer grim and saturnine, a silent man who regarded life chiefly as a test of endurance; but there is good authority for holding that "the best harmony is the resolution of discord," and of this aphorism the ill-matched pair offer an illustration. The friendship, as will be seen later, was of service to Schubert in more than one way.

As 1815 was the most prolific period of Schubert's life, so 1816 saw the first real change in his fortunes. Somewhere about the turn of the year Spaun surprised him in the composition of *Erlkönig*, Goethe's poem propped among a heap of exercise books, and the boy in the white heat of inspiration, hurling the notes onto the music paper.

A few weeks later Von Schober, a law student of good family and some means, who had heard some of Schubert's songs at Spaun's house, came to pay a visit to the composer and proposed to carry him off from school life and give him freedom to practice his art in peace.

The proposal was particularly opportune, for Schubert had just made an unsuccessful application for the post of Kapellmeister at Laibach, and was feeling more acutely than ever the slavery of the classroom. His father's consent was readily given, and before the end of the spring he was installed as a guest in Von Schober's lodgings. For a time he attempted to increase the household resources by giving music lessons, but they were soon abandoned, and he devoted himself to composition. "I write all day," he said later to an inquiring visitor, "and when I have finished one piece I begin another."

The works of 1816 include three ceremonial cantatas, one written for Salieri's Jubilee on June 16; one, eight days later, for a certain Herr Watteroth who paid the composer an honorarium of £4 ("the first time," said the journal, "that I have composed for money"), and one, on a foolish philanthropic libretto, for Herr Joseph Spendou, 'Founder and Principal of the Schoolmasters' Widows' Fund.'

Of more importance are two new symphonies, No. 4 in C minor, called the *Tragic*, with a striking andante, and No. 5 in B♭, as bright and fresh as a symphony of Mozart. There were also some pieces of church music, fuller and more mature than any of their predecessors, and over a hundred songs, among which are comprised some of his finest settings of Goethe and Schiller. There is also an opera, *Die Burgschaft*, spoiled by an illiterate book, but of interest because it shows how continually his mind was turned towards the theatre.

All this time his circle of friends was steadily widening. Mayrhofer introduced him to Vogl, the famous baritone, who did him good service by performing his songs in the salons of Vienna; Anselm Hüttenbrenner and his brother Joseph were among his most devoted admirers; Gahy, an excellent pianist, played his sonatas and fantasias; the Sonnleithners, a rich burgher family whose eldest son had been at the Convict, gave him free access to their home, and organized in his honour musical parties which soon took the name of *Schubertiaden*. The material needs of life were supplied without much difficulty.

No doubt Schubert was entirely penniless, for he had given up teaching, he could earn nothing by public performance, and, as yet, no publisher would take his music at a gift; but his friends came to his aid with true bohemian generosity — one found him lodging, another found him appliances, they took their meals together and the man who had any money paid the bill. Schubert was always the leader of the party, and was known by half-a-dozen affectionate nicknames, of which the

A 'Schubertiaden'

most characteristic was "kann er 'was?" his usual question when a new acquaintance was proposed.

1818, though, like its predecessor comparatively unfertile in composition, was in two respects a memorable year. It saw the first public performance of any work of Schubert's; an overture in the Italian style written as an admitted burlesque of Rossini, and played at a Jäll concert on March 1. It also saw the beginning of his only official appointment, the post of music-master to the family of Count Johann Esterhazy at Zelesz, where he spent the summer in pleasant and congenial surroundings.

The compositions of the year include a mass and a symphony, both in C major, a certain amount of four-hand piano music for his pupils at Zelesz and a few songs, among which are *Einsamkeit*, *Marienbild* and the *Litaney*.

On his return to Vienna in the autumn he found that Von Schober had no room for him, and he took up his residence with Mayrhofer. There his life continued on its accustomed lines. Every morning he began composing as soon as he was out of bed, wrote till two o'clock, then dined and took a country walk, then returned to composition or, if the mood took him, to visits among his friends.

He made his first public appearance as a songwriter on February 28, 1819, when the *Schäfers Klagelied* was sung by Jäger at a Jäll concert. In the summer of the same year he took a holiday and travelled with Vogl through Upper Austria.

At Steyr he wrote his brilliant piano quintet in A, and astonished his friends by transcribing the parts without a score. In the autumn he sent three of his songs to Goethe, but, as far as we know, received no acknowledgment.

The compositions of 1820 are remarkable, and show a marked advance in development and maturity of style. The unfinished oratorio *Lazarus* was begun in February; later followed, amid a number of smaller works, the 23rd Psalm, the *Gesang der Geister*, the Quartettsatz in C minor and the great piano fantasia *Der Wanderer*.

But of almost more biographical interest is the fact that in this year two of Schubert's operas appeared at the Kärnthnerthor theatre; *Die Zwillingsbrüder* on June 14, and *Die Zauberharfe* on August 19. Hitherto his larger compositions (apart from masses) had been restricted to the amateur orchestra at the Gundelhof, a society which grew out of the quartet parties at his home.

Now he began to assume a more prominent position and address a wider public. Still, however, publishers held obstinately aloof, and it was not until his friend Vogl had sung *Erlkönig* at a concert at the Kärnthnerthor (Feb. 8, 1821) that Diabelli hesitatingly agreed to print some of his works on commission. The first seven opus numbers (all songs) appeared on these terms; then the commission ceased, and he began to receive the meagre pittances which were all that the great publishing houses would ever give him.

Much has been written about the neglect from which he

Octet: sketch for a symphony

suffered during his lifetime. It was not the fault of his friends, it was only indirectly the fault of the Viennese public; the persons most to blame were the cautious intermediaries who stinted and hindered his publication.

The production of his two dramatic pieces turned Schubert's attention more firmly than ever in the direction of the stage; and towards the end of 1821 he set himself on a course which for nearly three years brought him continuous mortification and disappointment. *Alfonso und Estrella* was refused, so was *Fierrabras*; *Die Verschworenen* was prohibited by the censor (apparently on the ground of its title); *Rosamunde* was withdrawn after two nights, owing to the badness of its libretto.

Of these works the two former are written on a scale which would make their performances exceedingly difficult (*Fierrabras*, for instance, contains over 1000 pages of manuscript score). *Die Verschworenen*, however, is a bright attractive comedy, and *Rosamunde* contains some of the most charming music that Schubert ever composed.

In 1822 he made the acquaintance of both Weber and Beethoven, but little came of it in either case, though Beethoven cordially acknowledged his genius. Von Schober was away from Vienna; new friends appeared of a less desirable character; on the whole these were the darkest years of his life.

In the spring of 1824 he wrote the magnificent octet, *A Sketch for a Grand Symphony*; and in the summer went back to Zelesz, when he became attracted by Hungarian idiom, and wrote the *Divertissement à l'Hongroise* and the String Quartet in A minor.

Many biographers insert here a story of his passion for his pupil Countess Caroline Esterhazy; but whatever may be said as to the general likelihood of the romance, the details by which it is illustrated are apocryphal, and the song *l'Addio*, placed at its climax, is undoubtedly spurious.

A more debatable problem is raised by the grand duo in C major (D812) which is dated from Zelesz in the summer of this year. It bears no relation to the style of Schubert's piano music, it is wholly orchestral in character, and it may well be a transcript or sketch of the 'grand symphony' for which the octet was a preparation. If so, it settles the question, raised by Sir George Grove, of a 'Symphony in C major' which is not to be found among Schubert's orchestral scores.

Despite his preoccupation with the stage and later with his official duties, he found time during these years for a good deal of miscellaneous composition. The Mass in A♭ was completed and the exquisite "Unfinished Symphony" begun in 1822. The *Müllerlieder*, and several other of his best songs, were written in 1825; to 1824, beside the works mentioned above, belong the variations on *Trockne Blumen* and the two string quartets in E and E♭. There is also a sonata, for piano and 'arpeggione', an interesting attempt to encourage a cumbersome and now obsolete instrument.

The mishaps of the recent years were compensated for by the prosperity and happiness of 1825. Publication had been moving more rapidly; the stress of poverty was for a time lightened; in the summer there was a pleasant holiday in Upper Austria, where Schubert was welcomed with enthusiasm.

It was during this tour that he produced his *Songs from Sir Walter Scott*, and his piano sonata in A minor (D845), the former of which he sold to Artaria for £20, the largest sum which he had yet received for any composition. Sir George Grove, on the authority of Randhartinger, attributes to this summer a lost 'Gastein' symphony which is possibly the same work as that already mentioned under the record of the preceding year.

From 1826 to 1828 Schubert resided continuously in Vienna, except for a brief visit to Graz in 1827. The history of his life during these three years is little more than a record of his compositions. The only events worth notice are that in 1826 he dedicated a symphony to the Gesellschaft der Musikfreunde, which voted him in return an honorarium of £10, that in the same year he applied for a conductorship at the opera, and lost it by refusing to alter one of his songs at rehearsal, and that in the spring of 1828 he gave, for the first and only time in his career, a public concert of his own works.

But the compositions themselves are a sufficient biography. The string quartet in D minor, with the variations on *Death and the Maiden* (D810), was written during the winter of 1825-1826, and first played on Jan. 25. Later in the year came the string quartet in G major, the *Rondeau brilliant*, for piano and violin, and the fine sonata in G which, by some pedantry of the publisher's, is printed without its proper title.

To these should be added the three Shakespearian songs, of which *Hark! Hark! The Lark* and *Who is Sylvia?* were written on the same day, the former at a tavern where he broke his afternoon's walk, the latter on his return to his lodgings.

Franz Schubert.

In 1827 he wrote the *Winterreise*, the fantasia for piano and violin, and the two piano trios: in 1828 the *Song of Miriam*, the C major symphony, the Mass in E♭, and the exceedingly beautiful *Tantum Ergo* in the same key, the string quintet, the second Benedictus to the Mass in C, the last three piano sonatas, and the collection of songs known as *Schwanengesang*. Six of these are to words by Heine, whose *Buch der Lieder* appeared in the autumn.

Everything pointed to the renewal of an activity which could have equalled that of his greatest productivity, when he was suddenly attacked by typhus fever, and after a fortnight's illness died on Nov. 19 at the house of his brother Ferdinand. He had not completed his thirty-second year.

Some of his smaller pieces were printed shortly after his death, but the more valuable seem to have been regarded by the publishers as waste paper.

In 1838 Schumann, on a visit to Vienna, found the dusty manuscript of the Symphony in C major and took it back to Leipzig, where it was performed by Mendelssohn and celebrated in the *Neue Zeitschrift*.

The most important step towards the recovery of the neglected works was the journey to Vienna which Sir George Grove and Sir Arthur Sullivan made in the autumn of 1867. The account of it is given in Grove's appendix to the English translation of Kreissle von Hellborn; the travellers rescued from oblivion seven symphonies, the *Rosamunde* music, some of the masses and operas, some of the chamber works, and a vast quantity of miscellaneous pieces and songs. Their success gave impetus to a widespread public interest and finally resulted in the definitive edition of Breitkopf and Härtel.

Schubert is best summed up in the well-known phrase of Liszt; that he was *"le musicien le plus poète qui fut jamais."* In clarity of style he was inferior to Mozart, in power of musical construction he was inferior to Beethoven, but in poetic impulse and suggestion he is unsurpassed. He wrote always at headlong speed, he seldom corrected or changed anything, and the greater part of his work bears, in consequence, the essential mark of improvisation: it is fresh, vivid, spontaneous, impatient, full of both rich colour and imaginative feeling.

He was the greatest songwriter who ever lived, and almost everything in his hand turned to song. In his masses, for instance, he seems to chafe at the contrapuntal numbers, and pours out his soul on those which he found suitable for lyrical treatment. In his symphonies the lyric and elegiac passages are usually the best, and the most beautiful of them all is, throughout its two movements, lyric in character.

The standpoint from which to judge him is that of a singer who explored the whole field of musical composition and everywhere carried with him songwriting, the artistic form which he loved best.

Like Mozart, whose influence over him was always considerable, he wrote nearly all the finest of his compositions in the last ten years of his life. His early symphonies, his early quartets, even his early masses, are too much affected by a traditional style to establish an enduring reputation. It is unfair to call them imitative, but at the time when he wrote them he was saturated with Mozart, and early Beethoven, and he spoke what was in his mind with a boy's frankness. The *andante* of the Tragic Symphony (No. 4) strikes a more distinctive note, but the fifth is but a charming adaptation of a past idiom, and the sixth, on which Schubert himself placed little value, shows hardly any appreciable advance.

It is a very different matter when we come to the later works. The piano quintet in A major (1819) may here be taken as the turning point; then come the Unfinished Symphony, which is pure Schubert in every bar; the three quartets in A minor, D minor, and G major, full of romantic colour; the delightful piano trios; the great string quintet; and the C major symphony which, though diffuse, contains many passages of surprising beauty. Every one of them is a masterpiece, and a masterpiece such as Schubert alone could have written. The days of brilliant promise were over and were now succeeded by full and mature achievement.

His larger operas are marred both by their inordinate length and by their want of dramatic power. The slighter comedies are pretty and tuneful, but, except as curiosities, are not likely to be revived.

We may, however, deplore the fate which has deprived the stage of the *Rosamunde* music. It is in Schubert's best vein; the *entractes*, the Romance, and the ballets are all excellent, and it is much to be hoped that a poet will some day arise and fit the music to a new play.

Of his piano compositions, the sonatas, as might be expected, are the least enduring, though there is not one of them which does not contain some first rate work. On the other hand his smaller pieces, in which the lyric character is more apparent, are consistently interesting to play and pleasant to hear. He developed a special piano technique of his own, not always 'orthodox,' but always characteristic.

A special word should be added on his fondness for piano duets, a form which before his time had been rarely attempted. Of these he wrote a great many — fantasias, marches, polonaises, variations — all bright and melodious with sound texture and a remarkable command of rhythm.

His concerted pieces for the voice are often extremely difficult, but they are of a rare beauty which well repays the effort of rehearsal. The 23rd psalm (for female voices) is exquisite; so are the *Gesang der Geister*, the *Nachthalle*, the *Nachtgesang im Walde* (for male voices and horns), and that "dewdrop of celestial melody" which Novello has published with English words under the title of *Where Thou Reignest*. Among all Schubert's mature works there are none more undeservedly neglected than these.

Of the songs it is impossible, within the present limits, to give even a sketch. They number over 600, excluding scenes and operatic pieces, and they contain masterpieces from the beginning of his career to the end. *Gretchen am Spinnrade* was written when he was seventeen, *Erlkönig* when he was eighteen; then there follows a continuous stream which never checks or runs dry, and which broadens as it flows to the *Müllerlieder*, the Scott songs, the Shakespearian songs, the *Winterreise*, and the *Schwanengesang*.

He is said to have been undiscriminating in his choice of words. Schumann declared that "he could set a handbill to music," and there is no doubt that he was inspired by any lyric which contained, though even in imperfect expression, the germ of a poetic idea.

But his finest songs are almost all to fine poems. He set over

70 of Goethe's, over 60 of Schiller's; among the others are poems by Shakespeare and Scott, Schlegel and Rückert, Novalis and Wilhelm Müller — a list more than sufficient to compensate for the triviality of occasional pieces or the inferior workmanship of personal friends. It was a tragedy that he only lived for a few weeks after the appearance of the *Buch der Lieder*. We can only wonder what the world would have gained if he had found the full complement of his art in Heine.

In his earlier songs he is more affected by the external and pictorial aspect of the poem; in the later ones he penetrates to the centre and seizes the poetic conception from within. But in both alike he shows a gift for absolute melody which, even apart from its meaning, would be inestimable. Neither Handel nor Mozart — his two great predecessors in lyric tune — have surpassed or even approached him in fertility and variety of resource. The songs in *Acis* are wonderful; so are those in *Zauberflöte*, but they are not so wonderful as *Litaney*, and *Who is Sylvia?* and the *Ständchen*.

To Schubert we owe the introduction into music of a particular quality of romance, a particular "addition of strangeness to beauty"; and so long as the art remains, his place among its supreme masters is undoubtedly assured.

— *William Henry Hadow*

A young Franz Schubert

2

*Schubert's unique position among composers —
His birth and parentage — Early instruction in
music, and evidence of extraordinary talent —
Admission to the Imperial Chapel and Stadtconvict
— School experiences and first compositions —
Salieri — Symphony No. 1 in D — He decides to
leave the Convict.*

THERE ARE CIRCUMSTANCES in the personal career of
Franz Schubert, and in the history of his principal
works, which render his position among composers,
and indeed in art generally, peculiar, if not unique. He lived not
for himself, nor for those of his own time. This may be said of
many men of genius, who, misjudged and misunderstood by
their own generation, have afterwards come to be accounted
among the world's great.

But Schubert suffered less from opposition, prejudice, and
envy, than from simple lack of recognition. If we consider his
life in the abstract, it is that of an obscure individual who gained
a scanty livelihood first as a school teacher and afterwards as
a musician, who occupied his spare time with compositions of
all kinds which publishers looked upon with indifference,
grudgingly accepting a few towards the close of his life. There
is nothing here distinguishable from the experience of
numberless humble workers in any of the arts, who pursue
their useful but insignificant course, and vanish from sight and

Franz Theodore Schubert, father

memory at one and the same time.

Not for Schubert the varied experience among noble and princely patrons of music which Handel, Haydn, Mozart, and Beethoven enjoyed and suffered. Not for him the sunny existence of Mendelssohn, or the immediate popularity of Weber.

Life for him was commonplace, dreary, and even sometimes sordid; and yet, if we dwell for but an instant on the romantic and poetical in music, the name of Schubert is the first which rises to our lips. The mighty power of genius, defiant of circumstance and surroundings, was surely never better illustrated than in the master whose place and mission in the world we are discussing.

The Schuberts were natives of Zukmantel, in Austrian Silesia. Franz Theodore Schubert, the father, held an appointment as the parish schoolmaster of Lichtenthal, and became fairly comfortable in his vocation.

He first married Elizabeth Fitz, a cook, by whom he had fourteen children, of whom only five survived. These were named Ignaz, Ferdinand, Carl, Franz, and Therese. His wife died in 1812, and next year Franz the elder married Anna Klayenbök, the daughter of a mechanic, five more children being the result.

Elisabeth Schubert, mother

Franz Peter Schubert was born on January 31st, 1797, at Himmelpfortgrund No. 72, Lichtenthal, Vienna.

The elements of music are included in the curriculum of a German schoolmaster, and consequently young Franz found no hindrance in attaining the principles of the art towards which he manifested at the earliest age a remarkable predilection.

At first he was his own teacher, and when old enough to receive regular instruction, it was found that he had already mastered much of the groundwork of music.

At eight his father began teaching him the violin, and he could soon take his part in duets. He was then sent for singing lessons to Michael Holzer, the parish choirmaster, whose testimony in his favour is unqualified:

> "Whenever I wished to teach him anything new, I found that he had already mastered it. Consequently I cannot be said to have given him any lessons at all; I merely amused myself, and regarded him with dumb astonishment."

Ignaz Schubert, Franz's elder brother

His elder brother Ignaz taught him the piano; but after a few months Franz said that he did not require any more lessons, but would make his own way.

The evidence is therefore tolerably conclusive that Schubert showed extraordinary precocity in music, and if we do not read of any displays of his ability similar to those which gained for Mozart and Mendelssohn the wonder and admiration of persons outside the family circle, it is only because circumstances were not favourable to such manifestations.

Being possessed of a fine voice as a boy, he was admitted, early in 1808, into the parish church choir; and in October of the same year his father presented him as a candidate for admission to the Imperial Chapel, a position which included the right to education in the *Stadtconvict*.

It appears that his garb on this occasion was so abnormal, both in shape and colour, that the other competitors jokingly called him the 'miller's son.' But their laughter ceased when he began to sing, and the conductors, Salieri and Eybler, quickly recognising his ability, gave him preference.

He was now temporarily provided for, and his position was favourable to his advancement as a musician. In the school orchestra his ability soon brought him to the front, and he was made leader. Here he became acquainted with the symphonies of Haydn, Mozart, and Beethoven, together with those of other composers then popular but now forgotten. His greatest sympathies were shown towards those works which may be termed poetical and imaginative; thus he gloried in the G Minor Symphony of Mozart, which he declared was like the songs of angels, while his enthusiasm for Beethoven, then regarded by many as a mere dreamer, knew no bounds.

We have ample proof of the comparative poverty of the Schubert family at this time through the shortness of pocket money of which Franz complains. The following letter, addressed to his brother Ferdinand, illustrates this, and also affords a glimpse of the young musician's character:

> "You know by experience that a fellow would like at times a roll and an apple or two, especially if, after a frugal dinner, he has to wait for a meagre supper for eight hours and a half. The few *groschen* that I receive from my father are always gone to the devil the first day, and what am I to do afterwards ?

'Those who hope will not be confounded,' says the Bible, and I firmly believe it. Suppose, for instance, you send me a couple of *kreutzer* a month; I don't think you would notice the difference in your own purse, and I should live quite content and happy in my cloister.

St Matthew says also that 'whosoever has two coats shall give one to the poor'. In the meantime I trust you will lend your ear to the voice crying to you incessantly to remember your poor brother Franz, who loves and confides in you."

The boyish sense of fun which pervades this letter has a certain significance, for a vein of humour was conspicuous in Schubert's character to the very end.

One serious result of his poverty was the impossibility of purchasing music paper for the compositions which were now flowing in rapid succession; but this need was met by the generosity of one of his older schoolmates, Joseph Spaun, who had early recognised the genius of his friend.

Whether Franz had made any serious attempts at composition prior to his admission to the Stadtconvict cannot be distinctly ascertained; but in 1810 authentic records of his labours commence. In this year he wrote a piece for piano, for four hands, to which he gave the curious title *Leichenfantasie* (Corpse Fantasia), probably suggested by a poem of Schiller.

The manuscript bears the dates April 8 to May 1, 1810. It extends to 32 closely written pages, and consists of a dozen sections, in various styles, each ending in a key different to the one in which it commenced. Some variations for piano, also referable to this year, and played to his father, are stated by Ferdinand to bear the stamp of individuality.

In 1811 the list of compositions is much more extensive. It includes a quintet overture, a quartet, a fantasia for piano, and,

Antonio Salieri

of decidedly greater importance, his first songs, *Hagar's Klage* and *Der Vatermörder*.

Hagar's Klage is a remarkable piece, of the dimensions of a cantata, and, despite many crudities, is said to contain passages of a true Schubertian type. It at once drew the attention of Salieri to the boy's talent, and he was handed over to a musician named Ruczizka for lessons in harmony. The result was similar to that with Holzer. Ruczizka said:

> "He has learned everything, and God has been
> his teacher."

From Salieri, however, Schubert continued to receive instruction for some years, and his relations with this celebrated musician seem to have been generally satisfactory, and even cordial.

Antonio Salieri was for many years the most eminent of the

Italian musicians resident in Vienna. He was a man of very great ability, but he was wedded to the Italian school, and could neither comprehend nor sympathise with German musical development, which was now making rapid strides.

Hence, although his character was generally amiable, as the lasting attachment of his pupils — among whom were Hummel, Weigl, Moscheles, Meyerbeer — sufficiently indicates, his jealousy of Mozart made him stoop to mean and dishonourable intrigues against that great master; and a report was even circulated that he had poisoned him, the rumour gaining credence from the fact that poor Mozart in his last days suffered from delusions on the subject of poison. When Salieri was dying this horrible accusation troubled him, and he solemnly declared to Moscheles, who was by his bedside, his complete innocence of the crime.

There is, indeed, not a piece of evidence against him, but the very suspicion may be considered as just, if awful, retribution for the unworthy acts towards Mozart in which he had actually indulged.

It is not surprising that Salieri should have regarded with distrust the predilection of the young Schubert for the deep and imaginative utterances of the great German poets as material for the exercise of his musical creations; and it is equally natural that the boy, who felt the dawning power within him, should have totally disregarded his preceptor's advice to adopt Italian verses for his songs.

Still, with all his marvellous intuition, there can be little doubt that he derived benefit from the counsel and assistance of the old Italian maestro, particularly in the study of counterpoint and fugue.

It is time to return to Schubert's experiences while at the Convict. The compositions in 1812 are numerous, as will be seen by the catalogue. One song, *Klage*, is noteworthy as being the earliest of his compositions which have been published.

Ferdinand Schubert

The instrumental chamber works were played at home on holidays, the quartet being: Ferdinand, first violin; Ignaz, second violin; Franz, viola; and the father, cello.

Franz possessed much artistic sensitivity, and his quick ear detected the most trifling blunder. In the instance of one of his brothers he did not hesitate to rebuke either by word or look; but if his father played a wrong note or made a false entry he would ignore the mistake once, and if it occurred again he would say with hesitation, "Father, I fear there is a mistake somewhere..."

If a musician is asked to state in which branch of music Schubert was least successful, the unhesitating reply is "in music for the theatre." But this did not arise from want of sympathy, for he not only frequented the opera as often as circumstances would permit, but manifested the strongest enthusiasm for some of the masterpieces then in vogue. Weigl's *Swiss Family*, Cherubini's *Medée*, Boieldieu's *Jean de Paris*, Nicolos's *Cinderella*, and, above all, Gluck's *Iphigénie en Tauride* attracted him immensely, and as a result he began to feel a passion for dramatic composition.

In 1813, his last year at the Convict, he commenced work on Kotzebue's *Des Teufels Lustschloss*, which he completed in the following year. His first *Symphony in D* was composed in honour of the Convict director, Innocenz Lang, and, like his other orchestral works of this period, was performed by the school band. It is framed entirely on the Haydn-Mozart model, and consists of the usual four movements with an introductory *adagio*. The scoring is for the usual orchestra, without trombones and second flute.

The work has never been published, and the manuscript, dated October 28th, 1813, is in the possession of Dr. Schneider, in Vienna. On January 31st, 1880, the anniversary of Schubert's birthday, the first movement was performed at the Crystal Palace.

It proved to be a scholarly composition in the Mozart style, but showing traces also of the influence of Beethoven. Of individuality there is little or none, and the evidence of this and other early works indicates that Schubert's real genius began to manifest itself sooner in vocal than in instrumental composition, for some of his songs written at this time are in the highest degree expressive and original.

The piano minuets, composed for his brother Ignaz, elicited the remark from Dr. Anton Schmidt, an excellent musician, that

> "If these works are written by a mere child,
> there is the stuff in him to make a master such
> as few have been."

Unfortunately these pieces were not treated as they should have been, and the manuscripts were lost. The octet is marked in the catalogue of his compositions, kept by Ferdinand, as

Franz Schubert's Leickenfeier, possibly with reference to his mother's death, which took place a few months previously.

It is impossible within the limits of the present volume to comment on even a small proportion of Schubert's songs, which he poured forth with such wonderful rapidity. His style in this branch was already becoming matured, and his passion for the poetry of his native land is shown in his choice of authors. Those he selected this year were Schiller, Goethe, Matthison, Herder, Höltz, and Theodor Körner.

One Italian *aria* must also be mentioned, probably composed at the instigation of Salieri. Schubert was now in his seventeenth year, and his treble voice breaking, he had to leave the Imperial Chapel. His devotion to music had proven detrimental to his other studies. During his first year at school he passed his examinations creditably, but this satisfactory state of affairs did not last, and afterwards he gained commendations for only his musical progress.

He does not seem to have felt much anxiety on this score,

for he declined the privilege of staying on at the Convict for higher studies after his duties at the Chapel had ceased.

Music was the essence of his being, and, considering the vast quantity of works of all kinds which he penned during the brief period of eighteen years, it would have been surprising had he found time to pursue any other study to serious purpose. And it would be extremely idle and illogical to regret his concentration of energy on this one object. The world would would have lost had Schubert devoted the time occupied in writing down his music to perfecting himself in foreign languages or mathematics. He had a mission to accomplish, and the time allotted him was brief. Let us then be grateful that he fulfilled the task set before him so worthily and well.

One other point remains for consideration before we pass on to the next period in Schubert's life. It has been stated many times that he suffered from a lack of opportunities to hear his music performed. Whatever diffuseness, want of symmetry, or other defects may be discovered in his statements over the years can be attributed to this cause.

In his later years this was undoubtedly the case, but during his residence at the Convict, circumstances could hardly have been more favourable to his progress as a practicing musician. Both at school and at home, his songs and instrumental works were constantly performed, and the experience thus gained must have been of great value.

Later on, his theoretical studies under Salieri, whose attachment to rules and forms bordered on pedantry, must have had the effect of instilling a sense of mental discipline, a characteristic which remained with him for the rest of his life.

Schubert left the Convict at the close of October 1813, his residence there having lasted exactly five years.

3

Schubert's experience as a school teacher —
Friendship with Mayrhofer — Works from 1814;
Des Teufels Lustschloss, Mass in F, etc. —
Extraordinary productiveness in 1815 — Operas,
symphonies, masses, and songs — Characteristics
of Schubert's Lieder — Diary kept in 1816 — Der
Erlkönig — Cantatas and symphonies — He
applies for a position — Franz von Schober — He
leaves his father's school.

H E WAS NOW CAST ADRIFT in the world, confronted
with the necessity of earning his bread by the labour
of his own hands or brain. The financial circumstances
of his father precluded the possibility of Schubert devoting
himself exclusively to music until such time as his talents might
receive that recognition from both publishers and the public
which would grant him a position of independence.

The opportunity to assist in his father's school presented
itself, and he accordingly prepared himself for this drudgery
by studying for a term at the school of St. Anna.

Then for three years he settled down to an existence of
unspeakable dreariness, teaching the children of the poorer
classes of Vienna the alphabet and the rudiments of arithmetic.
How heartily he must have detested such an occupation can
well be imagined, but he performed his duties with unfailing
regularity and conscientiousness.

Only when he had to encounter an unusually stupid or obstinate child did his patience give way, and on such occasions he would administer chastisement with an unsparing hand.

If genius did not rise superior to all circumstances and conditions of life, we might feel surprised that the spirit of Schubert was not crushed by associations so degrading and wearisome; but in point of fact these years were not only among the most prolific of his life, but during them, he wrote some of those works which have made his name immortal.

The scanty evidence which remains to us regarding his personal character confirms that Schubert was naturally of a cheerful, even jovial, disposition, and keenly alive to the charms of society. After his lessons with Salieri, he would adjourn to a wine shop, and spend hours in conversation with his friends.

His capacity for forming friendships with his own gender is as remarkable as the poor record of his experiences with women. One attachment of the former kind was formed in

Johann Mayrhofer

1814, with the gifted but unhappy German poet Johann Mayrhofer.

In disposition this cynical, hypochondriac man, with his contempt and hatred of the world, and his inability to enjoy the pleasures of life because of his ceaseless contemplation of its pains, would seem to have little affinity with the gentle, easy-going, and shall we say — music apart — superficial, Schubert. But a mysterious bond of union may exist between two natures widely diverse in temperament, and it is certain that Mayrhofer and Schubert understood and sympathised with one another.

Their acquaintanceship was brought about by a mutual friend, who gave Schubert Mayrhofer's poem *To the Sea* to set to music. The musician then called upon the poet at his room, Wipplingerstrasse, No. 420, which they would afterwards share for two years.

Heinrich Grob

Another important relationship commenced in this year was that with Heinrich Grob and his sister, Therese.

The brother was skilful on the piano and the cello, and Therese had a beautiful voice, her singing being greatly admired by Schubert. He would frequently visit their house with his newest compositions, which they would rehearse with enthusiasm, greatly to the pleasure and advantage of the composer.

In the midst of his scholastic duties, and this social life in which he delighted, composition continued. The catalogue of his works in 1814 is sufficient for a decade of an ordinary composer's life.

First in order must be named the opera *Des Teufels Lustschloss*, which it will be remembered was commenced in the preceding year. The plot of this work is even more outrageous than that of Mozart's *Zauberflöte*, without the hidden significance and symbolism contained in Schikaneder's story. It deals with enchanted castles, monsters, deeds of daring, and all the paraphernalia of the romantic.

As a subject for an extravaganza it would pass well enough, but for a serious opera it is utterly ridiculous. Still Schubert's choice of such a theme demonstrates the innate love for the romantic and the mystical which is so conspicuous a feature in his work. No thought of public performance probably concerned him in setting Kotzebue's preposterous story; it offered him an opportunity of escape from the conventionalities of ordinary life, and he went to work with ardour, and with no other idea than that of exercising his ever-brimming imagination.

Of the music it is not possible to speak particularly, as it has not been published, nor indeed performed, except the overture. This is a bright and cleverly written piece, with an episode curiously resembling the passage with muted violins in Weber's *Euryanthe*. It is impossible that Weber can have been familiar with *Des Teufels Lustschloss*, and the likeness must be purely accidental, though it is curious, especially as each episode has reference to a supernatural event in the plot.

It is asserted that Schubert wrote two versions of this opera (or rather a play with incidental music), the one immediately succeeding the other. The revised score was shown to Salieri, who was delighted with the work; but this is rather doubtful evidence in its favour, as it is well-nigh certain that if the music

Therese Grob

THERESE GROB (16 November 1798 - 17 March 1875) was Schubert's first love. She was the daughter of Heinrich Grob and Theresia Männer (died 22 August 1826). She was born in Lichtental, Vienna. There was one other child, a boy called Heinrich (1800–1855) who was two years younger than Therese. The father died on 6 April 1804. The widowed mother continued to run the small silk-weaving business that Heinrich senior had established.

The premises were very near to Schubert's home. Therese had an attractive soprano voice, and her brother Heinrich was a talented pianist and violinist. The two families grew close through music-making. She often sang his latest songs, while a *Tantum ergo* and a *Salve Regina* were composed specially for her voice.

Therese sang in the Lichtental parish church, which Schubert had been attending since he was a child. For the church's centenary celebrations, the young Schubert completed his first mass in late July 1814 — the Mass in F, D105 — and Therese sang the soprano solo at the premiere performance, which Schubert conducted himself.

Her mementos of Schubert, including the songbook he compiled for her in 1816, were sequestered for many years by descendants of her nephew.

A Marriage Consent Law expressly forbade marriages by men in Schubert's class if they could not verify their ability to support a family. Schubert's application in April 1816, eventually rejected, for the post of music teacher at a teachers' training college in Ljubljana (then known as Laibach) may have been in part driven by his desire to gain some financial security to make marriage to Therese possible.

To Anselm Hüttenbrenner's question as to whether he had ever fallen in love, Schubert replied:

> "I loved someone very dearly and she returned my love. She was a schoolmaster's daughter, somewhat younger than myself, and she sang most beautifully and with great feeling. She was not exactly pretty and her face had pock-marks; but she had a heart, a heart of gold. For three years she hoped I would marry her; but I could find no position which would have provided for us both. She then later married someone else, which hurt me very much. I love her still, and no one since has ever appealed to me so much. But it seems she was not meant for me."

On 21 November 1820, Therese married Johann Bergmann (1797–1875), a baker. Together they had four children: Theresia (1821–1894), Johann Baptist (1822–1875), Amalia (1824–1886) and Carolina (b. 1828).

Schubert himself never married.

had been characterised by dramatic intensity of expression the old Italian would have condemned it as crude and unintelligible.

The fate of *Des Teufels Lustschloss* was unhappy. The composer eventually parted with the score to Herr Josef Huttenbrenner in payment of a trifling debt, and in 1848 some miserable domestic lit the fire with the second act. The first and third acts remain, but until the release of a complete edition of Schubert's works — an event to which musicians must look forward with eagerness — they are not likely to see the light.

Another and far nobler work composed in this year must now be spoken of. This is the Mass in F, the first, and with one exception the finest, he ever penned. It also has a special significance as having been the first composition intended for a public occasion, the centenary festival of the parish church of Lichtenthal.

Schubert conducted the performance in person, and Therese Grob sang the soprano part. It was afterwards repeated in the Church of St. Augustine, and Schubert's father, to mark his appreciation of his son's ability and progress, presented him with a five-octave piano.

Salieri's appreciation of the work was great and genuine. After the first performance he embraced Schubert, saying, "Franz, you are my pupil, and will do me great honour."

The composition of the mass lasted from May 17th to July 22nd, according to the dates on the manuscript. It remained unpublished until 1856.

The chief characteristics of the music are nobility, melodic beauty, and a true church-like style which, strangely enough, is wanting in some of the subsequent masses. The melody is as refined as that of Mozart, but the manner is totally diverse, and the most superficial listener could scarcely fail to detect the difference even if the work were performed with only piano

Mass No. 1 in F, D105.

accompaniment, while the orchestration has the true and unmistakable Schubertian stamp.

It would be a pleasant task to analyse the music of this period number by number; but it is sufficient as an indication of the young musician's power to cite the fugue *Cum Sancto Spiritu*, based on a bold subject and worked up to a resolution of surpassing grandeur.

The influence of Salieri's teaching is readily apparent, and it is easy to comprehend the delight which he showed at witnessing his pupil's mastery of the rules of composition.

The three quartets are in the Haydn-Mozart style, with just a trace here and there of Schubert's individuality.

The year 1815 brought no change in the placid, even monotonous, life of Schubert at this period, and it might be passed over altogether as being entirely uneventful, if it were not for the all-important fact that it was the most prolific of all with regard to composition.

Amazing as his rate of production was in previous years, all former efforts were eclipsed in 1815. Half a dozen dramatic works, two masses, two symphonies, a quantity of music for church and chamber, and nearly 150 songs together form the stupendous catalogue of works conceived and finished within the space of twelve months.

In the entire history of music, we can find no parallel to this inexhaustible fertility, and even if the entire mass had no artistic value, the mere physical labour expended in transferring the ideas from the brain of the composer to paper would testify to his industry.

It is certain that it was absolutely no trouble for Schubert to compose. The subject chosen, the ideas came naturally and abundantly without any expenditure of thought or energy. Unlike Mozart, he did not carefully perfect his works in his mind before writing them down; unlike Beethoven, he did not note his ideas in sketchbooks, and build up his music by a slow and careful process of selection and elaboration. Handel, Bach, and Haydn wrote with extreme rapidity, but not one of them exhibited fecundity similar to that of Schubert at the age of eighteen. Herr Spina has the manuscripts of seven songs, all composed on October 15th, 1815; and on the 19th four more were written.

Of the works in dramatic form, the first in order is *Der Vierjährige Posten*, an operetta in one act, written by Körner. The subject is lively and humorous, and quite suitable for light musical treatment. The music consists of a somewhat lengthy

A street scene in Vienna

overture and eight numbers. A bright soldiers' chorus was given with applause by the Vienna *Singverein* in 1860, but the work has never been performed on the stage.

The next is *Fernando*, a melodramatic piece by Albert Stadler, a contemporary of Schubert at the Convict. Schubert being possessed of a mania for operas just at this time, Stadler offered to compose a libretto, and did so, giving, as he said, a chief part "to thunder and lightning, grief and tears, as the favourite subjects of enthusiastic youth."

Schubert brought the completed score to Stadler in six days. They examined it together and then dismissed the subject from their minds. It is needless to add that it has never been performed on stage.

Claudine von Villabella by Goethe, is a more ambitious opera in three acts. The score came into the possession of Herr Hüttenbrenner, and the second and third acts shared the fate of the second act of *Des Teufels Lustschloss*; that is, servants tore them up to light fires during their master's absence in 1848. A complete copy of the work perished in the same way.

The music of the fragment yet remaining is said by Kreissle von Hellborn to be lacking in power, though characteristic and charming. The dramatic opportunities occur chiefly in the acts which are lost.

Die Beiden Freunde von Salamanka is the title of the next work which was written for Schubert by his friend Mayrhofer. This opera is on an extended scale, the score of the first act consisting of 320 pages. The libretto was not printed among Mayrhofer's poems, and it has been lost. The music, consisting of an overture and eighteen numbers, is said to contain only little of Schubert's individuality.

Besides these works there is evidence to show that he set Kotzebue's *Der Minnesinger* and *Der Spiegelritter*, and Mayrhofer's *Adrast*, but only fragments of the music remain. The net value of his writings for the stage in 1815 must be considered very small, though there are doubtless many songs and concerted pieces in these works which would be effective in the concert room.

Of greater interest are the two Symphonies in B♭ and D. These are both in the customary four movements, and are perfect as regards form. The scores are in the possession of Dr. Schneider, and neither work has ever been performed in Germany; but the symphony in B♭ was performed at the Crystal Palace on October 20th, 1877, and proved to be a bright and charming composition, showing the influence of Haydn rather than that of Mozart.

Of the two Masses in G and B♭, the first is dated March, and the second November.

The Mass in G was composed by Schubert for the Lichtenthal parish choir, especially for the pupils of his old master Hoker. In style it resembles the one in F, but is on a smaller scale and less varied. Curiously enough the Mass in B♭, which is distinctly inferior as church music to the earlier works, has hitherto enjoyed greater popularity, perhaps because of its resemblance to the well-known masses of Haydn and Mozart.

But the most remarkable feature of Schubert's activity this year is in the domain of songwriting. So far as can be ascertained, no less than 138 Lieder and ballads were written, and of these 83 have been published.

The number of these compositions is no less marvellous than their infinite variety. The source of inspiration seemed a matter of comparative indifference to him. He gathered his materials from all quarters, showing a preference, however, for lines in which longing or passionate yearning for some ideal were portrayed; and the appropriate musical expression came at once and as a matter of course.

Of course, not all his songs written at a particular period are of equal value. Side by side with some of the greatest beauty are others that are trifling and almost commonplace. But this much may be said; that when he had to set poetry of real power and significance, he rarely, if ever, failed to render justice to his theme. Perhaps the greatest charm in Schubert's songs is that they are perfectly lyrical, though intensely expressive.

To say that many of them are dramatic is to misuse that term. In order to realise this, it is only necessary to imagine some of his most picturesque works, such as *Die junge Nonne*, *Gretchen am Spinnrade*, or *Der Wanderer*, transferred to the stage. In this new atmosphere they would lose all their meaning, all their subtle power to charm.

The unpublished compositions include *Amphiaros*, by Komer, said to be a most effective declamatory song, and two ballads by a poet named Bertrand — *Minona*, and *Emma von Adelwald*. The latter is the most lengthy piece for a single voice that Schubert ever wrote.

The manuscript extends to 55 pages, and the music is fragmentary, some of the passages being very fine. Of a similar character is a setting of Höltz's *Die Nonne*. Herr Spina has possession of all these compositions, and they might with advantage be transferred to the list of published works.

1816 brought some slight relief from the daily round of drudgery to which Schubert had been subjected for three years. Circumstances also enable us to obtain a glimpse of the personal character, habits, and manner of thinking, of the young artist. The best means of gaining an insight to the character of someone is often the study of their diaries and private correspondence. Unhappily, this is only possible in the case of Franz Schubert to a very limited extent.

Whether Schubert was averse to letter writing there is no evidence one way or the other, but very little of his correspondence remains; and so one great asset which we find in the study of the lives of Mozart and Mendelssohn, and to a lesser extent of Beethoven and Weber, is denied to us. The remnants of his diaries that are still with us barely compensate for this loss.

It appears that he kept a daily record of his thoughts and experiences in 1816, but owing to that wanton carelessness with which Schubert's precious manuscripts seem to have been generally treated, only a small portion of these remain. Aloys Fuchs, in his *Schubertiana*, tells the story thus:

> "Some years ago I found at an autograph dealer's in Vienna the fragment of one of Schubert's diaries in his own handwriting, but several of the pages were missing. On my asking the reason of this, the wretched owner of the relic replied that he had for a long time been in the habit of distributing single pages of this manuscript to hunters of Schubert relics or autograph collectors. Having expressed my indignation at this vandalism, I took care to save what was left."

The pages that Fuchs rescued refer to four days only, and run as follows:

> *"June 13th, 1816.* This day will haunt me for the rest of my life as a bright, clear, and lovely one. Gently, and as from a distance, the magic tones of Mozart's music sound in my ears. With what alternate force and tenderness, with what masterly power, did Schlesinger's playing of that music impress it deep, deep in my heart.[1] Thus do these sweet impressions, passing into our souls, work beneficently on our inmost being, and no time, no change of circumstances, can obliterate them. In the darkness of this life they show a light, a clear, beautiful distance, from which we gather

---

[1] Schlesinger was an excellent violin player.

Crowding for a Schubert concert

confidence and hope. Oh, Mozart! Immortal
Mozart! How many and what countless images
of a brighter, better world have you stamped
on our souls! This quintet may be called one
of the greatest amongst his smaller works. I,
too, was moved on this occasion to introduce
myself. I played variations by Beethoven, sang
Goethe's *Rastlose Liebe* and Schiller's *Amalia*.
The first met with universal, the second with
qualified applause. Although I myself think my
Rastlose Liebe more successful than *Amalia*,
yet I cannot deny that to Goethe's musical
genius must be attributed, in a large measure,
the applause which greeted the song. I also
made the acquaintance of Madlle. Jenny, a
piano player with extraordinary powers of
execution, but I think her wanting in true and
pure expression.

June 14ᵗʰ, 1816. — After the lapse of a few months I took once more an evening walk. There can hardly be anything more delightful than of an evening, after a hot summer's day, to stroll about on the green grass. The meadows between Wahring and Dobling seem to have been created for this very purpose. I felt so peaceful and happy as my brother Carl and I walked together in the struggling twilight. 'How lovely!' I thought and exclaimed, and then stood still, enchanted. The neighbourhood of the churchyard reminded us of our excellent mother.

June 15ᵗʰ, 1816. — It usually happens that we form exaggerated notions of what we expect to see. At least I found it so when I saw the exhibition of pictures by native artists, held at Saint Anna. The work I liked best in the whole exhibition was a *Madonna and Child*, by Abel. I was much disappointed by the velvet mantle of a prince. I am convinced that one must see things of this sort much more frequently, and give them a longer trial, if one hopes to find and retain the proper expression and impression intended to be conveyed.

June 16ᵗʰ, 1816. — It must be pleasant and invigorating to see all one's pupils collected around him, every one striving to do his best in honour of his master's jubilee fête; to hear in all their compositions, a simple, natural expression free from all that *bizarrerie* which, with the majority of the composers of our time, is the prevailing element, and for which we are almost mainly indebted to one of our greatest German artists; free, I say, from that *bizarrerie* which links the tragic with the comic, the agreeable with the odious, the heroic with whining, the most sacred subjects with buffoonery — all this without discrimination; so that men become mad and frantic instead of being dissolved in tears, and tickled to idiotic laughter rather than elevated towards God...

Man is like a ball between chance and passion. I have heard it said by writers, 'The world is like a stage, where every man plays his part.' Praise and blame follow in the other world. Still every man has one part assigned to him — we have had our part given to us — and who can say if he has played it well or not?

Natural disposition and education determine the character of a man's heart and understanding. The heart is ruler; the mind should be. Take men as they are, not as they ought to be. Happy is he who finds a true friend. Happier still is he who finds in his own wife a true friend. To the free man at this time marriage is a fearful thought; he confounds it either with melancholy or low sensuality. Monarchs of our day, you see this and keep silence! Or do you not see it? Then, God, throw a veil over our senses, and steep our feelings in Lethe! Yet once I pray draw back the veil!

Man bears misfortune uncomplainingly; and for that very reason feels it all the more acutely. For what purpose did God create in us these keen sympathies? Light mind, light heart: a mind that is too light generally harbours a heart that is too heavy. Town politeness is a powerful hindrance to men's integrity in dealing with one another. The greatest misery of the wise man and the greatest happiness of the fool are based on conventionalism...

Now I know nothing more! Tomorrow I am sure to know something fresh! Whence comes this? Is my understanding today duller than it will be tomorrow? Because I am full and sleepy? Why does not my mind think when my body sleeps? I suppose it goes for a walk. Certainly, it can't sleep!"

It must be said that there is very little here of excellence in literary composition. The sudden subsidence into prose after the rhapsody on Mozart has an almost comical effect; and it is difficult to resist the idea that the disjointed philosophy of the latter portion was noted down after one of those potations in which Schubert was wont to indulge when the day's work was finished. That he felt deeply on the subject of music is certain; for the rest, he had no opportunity for mental cultivation except from his reading of the poets.

In regard to composition this year, the place of honour must go to those two songs which first made Schubert's name famous throughout the civilised world — *Der Erlkönig* and *Der Wanderer*. There are two versions of the first-named — one in the Royal Library, Berlin, and the other in the possession of Madame Schumann; the latter is identical with the song as we know it.

His friend Josef Spaun happened to call one afternoon and found him in intense excitement, working on Goethe's lines. The same evening the composer took the finished song to the Convict and tried it with his friends, who failed to appreciate the discord at the passage, "Mein vater, jetzt fasst er mich an."

But *Der Erlkönig* made its way in private, and five years later served to introduce Schubert to the notice of the outside world. The total number of songs, parts of songs, and other small vocal

Der Erlkönig

pieces written this year is about 120, of which 60 are published.

On June 16th, Salieri completed his fiftieth year of service to the Emperor of Austria, and at a friendly gathering of his pupils a cantata by Schubert, among other compositions, was performed. It was a *pièce d'occasion*, and remains unpublished.

Of far greater value was the cantata *Prometheus*, written for the birthday of Professor Watteroth. This was the first commission ever given to Schubert, and he received 100 florins for his labours. The performance made a deep impression, and the work was repeated several times in his later years; but about the time of his death the score disappeared and has never been recovered. A third cantata was composed in honour of Josef Spendou, Inspector of Schools, and afterwards published as Opus 128 (D472).

Among the compositions for Church are the rather superficial Mass in C, a grand Magnificat in C, of which Herr Spina has the manuscript, and a second *Stabat Mater* in F minor, said to be a very fine work.

The only dramatic piece of the year was an opera entitled *Die Bürgschaft* of which only two acts were finished. The author of the libretto is unknown, and the words are frequently criticised. This piece has ever been performed in public.

The list of instrumental music is important, including, as it does, two symphonies — the melodious and agreeable No. 4 in Bb (without trumpets or drums), and the beautiful *Tragic* in C minor. These works are published only as piano duets, but they have both been heard at the Crystal Palace in their full form, and the latter especially is enjoyed by Schubert's admirers.

The quartet parties which had been held in Schubert's house had by this time increased in numbers, and were transferred first to Herr Franz Frischling's, and afterwards to the house of Herr Otto Hatwig. Orchestral music was gradually introduced, and it was for these assemblies that Schubert wrote the two symphonies just mentioned, as well as other works for orchestra and chamber. He had to accommodate himself to the varying means at his disposal, and this accounts for the absence of clarinets, trumpets, and drums in the Symphony in Bb.

In April of this year Schubert made an application for the post of music master at the Normal School Institute, Laibach. The salary offered was 500 florins. He gained testimonials from Spendou and Salieri, but the latter, who had to examine the candidates for the office, recommended a certain Jacob Schaufl as the most suitable person for the duties.

Franz von Schober

Thus foiled, he had to resume his drudgery; but another opportunity for freedom soon presented itself. Franz von Schober, a student at Vienna University, became acquainted with some of his songs, and being struck with their beauty and originality sought out the composer, and was amazed when he discovered the conditions under which the young musician produced such noble creations. He thereupon gained the consent of his own mother and of Schubert's father for the composer to live with him so that he might pursue his art without let or hindrance.

According to one story, however, Schubert was dismissed from the school for having administered too severe a chastisement to one of the pupils. The truth of this is not known, but it is certain that he left his father's house for that of Schober, though the date when this occurred is unknown.

Liechtental Church was Schubert's childhood church, just a couple of blocks from both his childhood home and his brother Ferdinand's house, where he died. His parents were married here, and he himself was baptized here. Schubert was organist here for ten years, and this is where two of his masses were premiered.

This new friendship was destined to exercise considerable influence on Schubert's career, and of all his friends and patrons, Franz von Schober stands foremost for the countenance and support given to Schubert until his death.

Schubertiade, evenings of Schubert's music
with the composer playing, were popular.

Schubert's father's schoolhouse.
Schubert taught here from 1814 to 1816.

4

*Johann Michael Vogl — Josef Hüttenbrenner —
Piano sonatas — Overtures in the Italian style —
He becomes music teacher to the Esterhazy family
— His residence with Mayrhofer — Excursion in
upper Austria — Rossini — Goethe — His first
commissions for the stage — Die Zwillingsbrüder
— Die Zauberharfe — Contemporary criticism —
The oratorio Lazarus — The Fantasia in C.*

I F SCHUBERT WAS UNFORTUNATE in his relations with the
world in general, and with music publishers in particular,
he was happy in his personal relationships.

About this time he made the acquaintance of Johann Michael
Vogl, the most celebrated baritone singer of his time, and a man
greatly superior to the majority of singers on account of his
natural intellectual gifts, early and rigorous mental training,
and a capacity for comprehending the world around him in all
its varied phases. The introduction to Vogl was brought about
by Schober, whose constant lauding of Schubert at length
overcame the reluctance, generally felt by vocalists, to have
any dealings with a new and untried composer.

At the first meeting Schubert's awkward and bashful
manner did not improve matters, and Vogl's remarks, after
examining some of his songs, were patronising rather than
encouraging. But his appreciation of their value was genuine,
and as it rapidly increased with further acquaintance, he began

Johann Michael Vogl

to sing them both in public and in private. This was just the opportunity which Schubert needed, but thanks to his own backwardness and publishers' shortsightedness, several years were yet to elapse before it began to bear fruit.

In the summer of this year he made the acquaintance of Josef Hüttenbrenner, whose name has already been mentioned. The unfortunate destruction of some of Schubert's scores in his possession must not be taken as proof of his lack of appreciation of the composer's genius. On the contrary, he was an ardent admirer of the gifted musician, and expressed his opinion so strongly, in season and out of season, that Schubert, who was usually insensible to flattery, treated him with rudeness, exclaiming on one occasion, "Why, that man likes everything I do!"

Josef Hüttenbrenner

But Hüttenbrenner's praise was not lightly given nor valueless, for he was himself a cultured musician, and rendered Schubert considerable assistance with arranging his orchestral works for the piano, in his communications with foreign publishers, and in other labours of a kind most distasteful to the composer.

The exact position of Schubert during most of 1817 is a matter of some doubt; but as regards productivity, his release from the duties of teaching does not seem to have had the effect intended by Schober, for there is a considerable falling off in the bulk of his writings this year.

The deficiency in mere extent and number, however, is amply atoned for, even if we reject the statement that the fine piano sonatas in D (D850), in A (D664), in E♭ (D568), in A minor (D784), and in B (D575), were all created at this time. This is so according to Reissmann, but Nottebohm in his *Thematische Verzeichniss* names 1823 as the probable year of the A Minor Sonata, and 1825 as that of the works in D and A.[1]

---

[1] Ereissle speaks of Sonatas in A♭ and F;
according to Nottebohm these are fragments.

Internal evidence goes far to prove that Nottebohm is nearer the truth; but the sonatas in E♭, B, and A minor (D537), are works of great beauty, and they are supplemented by the trio for strings in B♭, and the two sonatas for violin and piano Nos. 1 (D384) and 2 (D385). The trio is still unpublished, but a copy was brought to this country by George Grove in 1867, and it was performed on February 15th, 1869, at the Monday Popular Concerts.

Orchestral music is solely represented by the two 'overtures in the Italian style' in C and D. These overtures afford yet another instance of the strange insensibility of one musical genius towards the work of another. Handel on Gluck, Weber and Spohr on Beethoven, Weber on Schubert, Schumann on Meyerbeer, and many living musicians on Wagner; all furnish examples of a lack of appreciation where sympathy and admiration might be expected.

Schubert, with all his nonchalance and lightheartedness, probably felt some vague jealousy towards Rossini, whose works were at the time enjoying high favour in Vienna. One evening after hearing *Tancredi*, some of his friends waxed loud in praise of Rossini's overtures, and Schubert contemptuously remarked that it was the easiest thing in the world to write music in that style. By way of proof, he produced at once the Overture in D, and a few months later the one in C.

It may be said that the last named work does reflect some of the mannerisms of Italian music, but it cannot be considered as equal to the work of Rossini.

Some time during 1817, Schubert ceased to receive instruction from Salieri. It says much for the personality of the Italian master that he was able to retain as his pupil for so long one so opposed to him in temperament and manner of thinking as the composer of the *Erl King*. The final separation of the two seems to have been abrupt and attended with some unpleasantness, but the exact circumstances remain unknown.

The Esterhazy estate at Zelesz today.

In the summer of 1818, Schubert received an offer which, to one who had no regular income, was too good to refuse. Count Johann Esterhazy required a music teacher for his family. The remuneration was to be two gulden a lesson, and Schubert was to reside with the family; in winter at Vienna, and in summer at the country seat, Zelesz.

It is easy to imagine that he readily agreed with this offer, which, apart from the actual work of teaching, presented a prospect that was highly pleasing, as well as profitable. The Count's family consisted of himself and wife, their daughters Marie and Caroline, aged respectively thirteen and eleven, and a boy of five years.

The entire family was musically disposed, and one of their most frequent visitors was Baron Carl von Schönstein, the finest amateur singer of his time. This gentleman, initially an adherent of the Italian school, became an ardent lover of Schubert's songs, which he sang everywhere, and in doing so assisted in spreading appreciation of Schubert's work.

Baron Carl von Schönstein

That Schubert's position with the Esterhazys was considered a highly favourable one is apparent from the following part of a letter written by his brother Ignaz:

> "You lucky mortal, what a thoroughly enviable lot is yours!
>
> To live in a sweet golden freedom; you can give full play to your musical genius; scatter your thoughts about just as you please; become petted, praised, idolised, whilst one of our lot, like an old cart-horse, must put up with all the vagaries of noisy boys, submit to heaps of ill-usage, and cringe in submission to a thankless public and addle-pated superstitious Brahmins."

The score for *Die Forelle* (The Trout). D.667.

The composer now had a direct incentive to exercise his genius, and many of his compositions were made possible by the Esterhazys. There is no evidence, however, to indicate that any of the productions of 1818 were written for his new patrons.[1] Chief among the comparatively small list is the bright and beautiful Symphony in C (No. 6), the score of which is dated February, 1818. With reference to a favourite song, *Die Forelle*, he wrote thus to Josef Hüttenbrenner:

> "Dearest friend, I am overjoyed to find that my songs please you. As a proof of my sincere friendship, I send you another which I wrote at midnight for Anselm. But what mischief! Instead of the box of blotting-sand, I seized the ink bottle. I hope, over a glass of punch at Vienna, to become better acquainted with you. Vale! – *Schubert.*"

---

[1] Reissmann gives 1818 as the date of the *Divertissement à la Hongroise* and the *Variations on a French Air*; but this is at variance with Nottebohm, and probably incorrect.

For some reason which does not appear, the arrangement that he should reside with the Esterhazy family seems to have fallen through, for early in 1819 we find him back in Vienna, sharing a gloomy, ill-furnished room with the poet Mayrhofer.

The way of life of the two was thoroughly bohemian. The following is an entry from Mayrhofer's diary.

> "Whilst we were together curious things happened. We certainly were both of us peculiar, and there were plenty of opportunities for droll incidents. We used to tease one another in all sorts of ways, and bandied pleasantries and epigrams for our mutual benefit. His free, open-hearted, cheerful manner and my retired nature came into sharp contact, and gave us an opportunity of nicknaming each other appropriately, as though we were playing certain parts assigned us. Alas! It was the only role I ever played."

The method in which this singular pair pursued their creative work was unique. Mayrhofer would sit at his desk and write some stanzas, and then toss them over to Schubert, who would immediately commence to set them to music without the slightest hesitation.

The poet's reference to Schubert's "free, open-hearted, cheerful manner" must be accepted with some reservation. In private Schubert may have been as Mayrhofer has reported, but in his dealings in business, and with those who could have advanced his interests as a musician, his manner was awkward, retiring, and even almost clownish.

In the summer of 1819 he accompanied his friend and adviser, Vogl, on a short tour in the beautiful region of Upper Austria, visiting Linz, Salzburg, and Steyr (Vogl's birthplace). It is probable that the singer defrayed more than his own share of the expenses on this and subsequent excursions.

The score for *Trost*, D671.
Music by Schubert, words by Johann Mayrhofer.

Vogl introduced his companion to several musical families at Steyr, and he seems to have spent a pleasant time. A letter dated July 15th to his brother Ferdinand indicates his state of mind, as does the following, addressed to Mayrhofer from Linz:

> "August 19th. My dear Mayrhofer, if the world thrives as well with you as it does with me, you are well and hearty. I am just at present in Linz. I have been with the Spauns, and met Kenner, Kriel, and Forstmayer. There, too, I made acquaintance with Spaun's mother, and Ottenwald, whose *Cradle* song I set and sang to him. I found plenty of amusement in Steyr. The surrounding country is heavenly, and Linz too is beautiful. We, that is, Vogl and I, shall go very soon to Salzburg.

Johann Michael Vogl

How I long for —!

I recommend to your notice the bearer of this letter, a student of Kremsmünster, of the name of Kahl; he is journeying by way of Vienna to Idria on a visit to his parents. Please let him have my bed during the time he stays with you. I am anxious that you should treat him as kindly as possible, for he is a dear good fellow. Please greet Frau v. S. heartily for me.

Have you written anything? I hope so. We celebrated Vogl's birthday with a cantata, the words by Stadler, the music by me; people were thoroughly pleased.

Now, then, farewell, until the middle of September.

Your friend,
Franz Schubert."

Franz Jäger

About this time 'Rossini fever' was rising rapidly in Vienna, and Franz was frequently at the Italian opera, for his nature was too open and candid to deny altogether the genius of the brilliant composer, though his admiration is expressed in rather qualified terms. In a letter to a friend in Gratz, he says:

> "A short time ago we had Rossini's *Othello*. All that our Radichi executed was admirable. This opera is far better, I mean more characteristic, than *Tancredi*. One cannot refuse to call Rossini a rare genius; his instrumentation is often original in the highest degree, and so is the voice-writing, and I can find no fault with the music, if I except the usual Italian gallopades, and several reminiscences of *Tancredi*."

It was during this year that for the first time a song of Schubert's was introduced at a public concert. Franz Jäger, a tenor, sang *Schäfers Klagelied* on two occasions, and it was received with much applause, but the publishers remained as obtuse as ever.

Johann Goethe

In another quarter, too, where he might indeed have looked for sympathy and admiration, he met with coldness and indifference. Urged probably by some well-meaning friend, he sent some of his settings of Goethe's songs to the great poet himself, who set them aside without a reaction of any kind.

It is well known that Goethe was unable to appreciate *Der Erlkönig* until late in life when he heard the great Schroeder-Devrient sing it. He was profoundly impressed, saying:

The courtyard of the Schubert family home. In the right foreground is the pool of the 'Trout' Quintent, D667.

> "I once heard this composition in my earlier
> life, and it did not agree with my views of the
> subject, but, executed as you execute it, the
> whole becomes a complete picture."

The fact seems to be that Goethe, strange as it may appear, had no feeling for the romantic in music, his favourite songwriter being Zelter, who set more than a hundred of his poems as flowing rhythmical ballads.

The most important composition this year was the Quintet for Piano and Strings (D667). The cantata mentioned in his letter from Linz as beingwritten for Vogl's birthday, was published with new words in 1849 under the title of *Der Frühlingsmorgen* (D666). It is for soprano, tenor, and bass, with piano accompaniment.

There is an Overture in F for piano, for four hands, "written in November in Herr Josef Hüttenbrenner's room, at the City Hospital, within the space of three hours, and dinner missed in consequence." Kreissle speaks of this as being in F minor, but the introduction only is in the minor key.

The year 1820 is one of far greater interest in the matter of composition. Now we find Schubert once more writing for the stage, but not, as before, merely for his own will and pleasure.

His friend Vogl had for a long time been unflagging in his efforts to secure recognition for the gifted young musician, and at length succeeded in inducing the management of the Kärnthnerthor Theatre to give Schubert a small commission; to set to music a farcical piece entitled *Die Zwillingsbrüder*, adapted from the French by Hofmann, the secretary of the theatre. It would seem that he commenced work as early as 1818, at any rate the overture bears the date January 19, 1819; but the composition went only slowly, for Schubert had now become more careful in his choice of subjects, and *Die Zwillingsbrüder* failed to interest him.

Hence the music is on the whole scarcely worthy of him, though agreeable and melodious. The piece was produced on June 14th 1820, and the impression created was favourable, for the chorus *Vergluhet sind die Sterne* was encored, and at the close there was a call for the composer. Vogl appeared in his stead, and expressed his thanks to the audience.

The critics damned the work with faint praise, admitting that the composer had ability, and that his music showed the result of careful study, but that it was old-fashioned and deficient in melody. The *Allgemeine Musikalische Zeitung* stated its opinion:

> "The work is deficient in real melody, and the music suffers from a confused overladen instrumentation, a painful effort after originality, constant wearisome modulations, and no intervals for repose. The introductory chorus, a quartet, and a bass air, alone entitle us to cling to the hope of a brilliant future for a young man already known to fame from his clever songs, and for this future he has yet to

win the necessary self-dependence and solid
powers required to form a real composer."

The writer of this review seems to have been unaware that
the musician whom he thus lectured so calmly was already the
composer of two splendid masses, several charming
symphonies, together with piano and chamber works sufficient
to ensure a lasting reputation for their author. *Die
Zwillingsbrüder* was repeated six times, and then laid aside,

never to be revived. The score was published in 1872.

Schubert, however, was asked to compose another dramatic piece in three acts, entitled *Die Zauberharfe*. The libretto by Hofmann is incredibly stupid, and part of the failure of the work must be ascribed to this cause. But Schubert himself considered it one of his best works, and if the music generally is equal in merit to the overture — now known as *Rosamunde* — his opinion is correct. Unfortunately, no complete copy of the score is known to exist. Portions of the music are in possession of Spina and Spaun, but the only published piece is the overture already mentioned.

Die Zauberharfe was produced on August 19th, and repeated several times; but like *Die Zwillingsbrüder* it soon disappeared, and was never heard of again. The following criticism is from the *Allgemeine Musikalische Zeitung*:

> "The composer gives glimpses here and there of talent; but there is on the whole a want of technical arrangement, which can only be gained by experience; the numbers, generally speaking, are too long and wearisome; the harmonic progressions too harsh; the instrumentation overladen, the choruses vapid and weak. The most successful numbers are the introductory Adagio of the overture, and the romance for the tenor; the expression of these is lovely, the simplicity is noble, and the modulation delicate. An idyllic subject would be admirably adapted to the composer."

Some of the remarks here and in the previous extract are similar in tone to those often adopted by shallow critics towards new composers of genius, from Mozart to Wagner.

But when we find other writers complaining that:

> "...the musical treatment hindered rather than helped the action, and betrayed the absolute ignorance on the part of the composer of the rules of the melodrama..."

and further that

> "...the music for the magic harps was wanting in the necessary power and characteristics which ought always to accompany ethereal spirits,"

we are constrained to believe that Schubert in this, as in other instances, showed little regard for the exigencies of stage composition; that, in short, he poured forth all the products of his imagination without consideration for the modifications of style and structure absolutely essential in music intended to accompany and illustrate the action of a drama. It was singularly unfortunate that he should be first brought to the notice of the Viennese musical public in the branch of music in which he was least original and successful.

Meanwhile he had been for some time engaged on a work of far greater interest and importance, and which, like the majority of his masterpieces, was the fruit of his own fancy, and not induced by pressure from without.

In 1814 there appeared a volume of sacred poems by August Hermann Niemeyer, chancellor of the Halle University. Among these was one on the death and resurrection of Lazarus, and this Schubert commenced to set to music, the circumstances of the composition, and even its very existence, being entirely unknown to his closest friends.

For its ultimate discovery we are indebted to Kreissle von Hellborn, who, in collecting materials for his biography, came across the first part of *Lazarus* in Spaun's collection. A portion of the second part was found in the possession of Mr. Alexander

Thayer, and some additional pieces in that of Ferdinand Schubert's widow. Still the second part remains incomplete, and of the third not a trace has been found.

This is to be regretted, as this section of the poem contains the incident of the resurrection, which would have given Schubert a magnificent opportunity to exercise his genius. The fragment was published by Spina in 1866, and it deserves to take rank among Schubert's noblest choral works. There is no reason to dwell here in detail on the music, as it is readily available to those who may desire its acquaintance.

Beside these works there is an unfinished opera entitled *Sakontala*, based on a romantic and supernatural Indian subject. Only one number, a celestial chorus, is complete, but the whole of the two acts is sketched out. Josef Hüttenbrenner says that neither Schubert nor his friends liked the libretto, and it was therefore laid aside.

The beautiful psalm *The Lord is my Shepherd* was written for four sisters named Fröhlich.

The composer was not himself a wonderful performer on the piano, though he accompanied his own songs with perfect expression, and fairly mastered the sonatas. But the magnificent Fantasia in C, *The Wanderer* (D760), was too much for him, and one occasion, on attempting it at a private party, he broke down in the finale, and jumping up from his chair, exclaimed "The devil may play the stuff if he likes!"

Franz Schubert

Am. 10 July 1821

5

The first publications — Enthusiasm of his friends — Schubertiaden — The symphony in E — Schubert and Beethoven — Alfonso and Estrella; performance at Weimar — The mass in A♭ — The unfinished symphony in B minor — Schubert and Weber — Rosamunde — Fierabras — Die Verschwornen, or Der häuslicne Krieg — Die schöne Müllerin — Publications in 1823.

THE YEAR 1821 may be considered the turning point in Schubert's career. We have seen how a couple of operettas were performed at the Kärnthnerthor Theatre, and that after a glimpse of success they were withdrawn from the repertoire. It was not in the field of dramatic music that he could hope to find general acceptance.

But his enthusiastic and sincere friends worked steadily on his behalf, and at length succeeded in getting his name before the public in the most favourable light — that is, as a songwriter. Among this select band of patrons was the Sonnleithner family.

Dr. Ignaz von Sonnleithner and his son Leopold were cultured musicians, and their house was visited by many interested in the art. Performances were held at regular intervals, and Schubert's music appeared in these programmes more and more frequently.

At length Leopold von Sonnleithner took *Der Erlkönig* to the

Dr. Ignaz von Sonnleithner

publishers Diabelli and Haslinger, who both refused it on any terms, alleging that the composer was almost unknown, and the accompaniment too difficult!

Thus foiled, he secured the assistance of three others, and the song was printed by subscription, Diabelli publishing it on commission. Sales were good, and Schubert was able to pay his debts and have some left over.

On March 7th, Ash Wednesday, an important concert was given at the Kärnthnerthor Theatre, and three of Schubert's compositions were included in the programme. Vogl sang *Der Erlkönig* and was rapturously encored. The other pieces were a quartet, *Das Dörfchen*, and the *Gesang der Geister über den Wassern*. This poem of Goethe had been set in 1817 as a male voice quartet without accompaniment. A second arrangement for four tenors and four basses, with viola, cello, and bass accompaniment was nearly completed in December 1820, and the final version, differing only slightly from this, was the one performed on March 7th.

The work is one of Schubert's noblest inspirations, but it is undeniably sombre, and suggestive of Beethoven in his darker mood. Carefully rehearsed, and sung with great earnestness, it failed to please the audience, and, as Kreissle states,

> "...the eight victims on the altar of musical insensibility withdrew in confusion from the scene, looking very much as if they were shivering from the effects of cold water suddenly poured over their heads..."

The enlightened critic of the *Allgemeine Zeitung* says:

> "The eight-part chorus by Herr Schubert was recognised by the public as a farrago of all sorts of musical modulations and vague departures from ordinary forms — no sense, no order, no meaning. The composer, in such works, resembles a wagon driver with a team of eight horses, which he turns now to the right, now to the left, getting at one time out of the road, then upsetting, and pursuing this game without once making any honest way."

It will be seen by reference to Nottebohm's *Thematische Verzeichniss* that no less than eighteen songs were published this year, extending from Opus 1 to 7. The business arrangements, even down to the dedications, were undertaken for the most part by friends, for Schubert had no idea about business matters.

The devotion shown towards him at all times by a few choice spirits, who, by natural temperament or an intuitive perception of his qualities, were drawn into the magic circle of his genius, was as remarkable as the blindness and indifference shown by those whose position gave them power and influence to forward, or not, the interests of a young and gifted musician.

That Schubert reciprocated this feeling is undoubted; but his light and unsophisticated nature led him to receive more readily the sympathy of young men of his own age and habits than the more staid, but no less sincere, appreciation and efforts of persons who were enabled by their social footing to work more effectively in his interests.

Had he lived to witness and enjoy the fruits of his intellect and imagination from a position of comfort and independence, that eminence would not have been attained by his own personal tact and energy; he had as little of courtier-like qualities and worldly-mindedness as Beethoven, although with his close friends he was more amenable to the influences of genial fellowship than Beethoven.

One of his most steadfast friends was Franz von Schober, with whom, in the summer of this year he made an excursion to the village of Ochsenburg on the slopes of the Styrian mountains. This visit resulted in the composition of the opera *Alfonso and Estrella*, of which Schober wrote the libretto. As this work was not finished until the succeeding year we shall defer for the present any remarks upon it.

A letter to Spaun written on November 2nd throws some light on Schubert's position and feelings at this time.

> "Dear Friend, your letter has pleased me very much, and I trust you will always be happy and comfortable. I must now, however, inform you that my dedications have done their duty, for the Patriarch, at the instance of Vogl, has expended twelve ducats, and Friess twenty — a fact which suits me extremely well. You must also be so kind as to conclude your correspondence with the Patriarch by a

Franz von Schober

Joseph Spaun

suitable acknowledgement made to him and me also. Schober's opera has already got to the third act, and I should much like you to have been present whilst the opera was in its earliest stage of formation. We count a good deal on the work in question. The Kärnthnerthor and Wiedner Theatres are actually leased to Barbaja, and his lease begins to run next December. Now farewell. Remember me to all friends, particularly your sisters and brothers. Your friend, Franz Schubert."

The 'patriarch' here mentioned was Ladislaus Pyrker, a poet of some standing, whose stanzas *Die Allmacht* and *Das Heimweh* Schubert set to music.

Around this time, social events known as *Schubertiaden* were organised by the friends and admirers of the young musician. At these lively gatherings there were speeches, songs, dances, and conviviality, the music always consisting of Schubert's own compositions. Here he was in his element, surrounded by congenial and sympathetic companions, and utterly careless as to the present and the future — as if, indeed, some inward monitor told him that whatever trials and troubles were in store, his deathless fame was secure.

Later on, as we shall see, he suffered from depression; but during this period there is nothing to indicate that he was anything but cheerful and lighthearted — a condition arising as much from his natural buoyancy as from his improved worldly prospects.

Beside the first and second acts of *Alfonso and Estrella* the record of composition in 1821 is a small one.

The most important item is the sketch of the Seventh Symphony in E, which for some inexplicable reason was allowed to remain in its incomplete state. This sketch came

A Schubertiade

into the possession of Ferdinand Schubert, who presented it to Mendelssohn in 1845 or 1846. When Mr. George Grove made his memorable pilgrimage to Vienna in 1867 he was induced by the references to this symphony in Kreissle's biography to search for it, in order, as he expresses it, to make up the magic number of nine.

We cannot do better than quote Mr. Grove's own words regarding this imperfect but precious relic. He says:

> "I was at length rewarded by receiving in August last, from Mr. Paul Mendelssohn of Berlin, the brother of the composer, the original manuscript sketch which I had so anxiously desired.

I had imagined a sketch of the nature of Beethoven's — two or three leaves of paper covered with disjointed memoranda. Imagine my astonishment and delight when on unfolding the parcel, I found a whole symphony in 44 sheets.

It is one of the most singular and interesting works in all of music.

The Introduction and a portion of the Allegro are fully scored and completed, but at the 110th bar (the end of a page) Schubert appears to have grown impatient of this regular proceeding, and from that point to the end of the Symphony he has made merely memoranda. But these memoranda are perfectly orderly and intelligible. Every bar is drawn in through the entire work; the *tempi* and names of the instruments are fully written at the beginning of each movement: the very double bars and flourishes are gravely added at the end of each, and *Fine* at the conclusion of the whole; and Schubert evidently regarded the work as completed.

And so it practically is, for each subject is given at full length, with a bit of bass, or accompaniment, or figure or fugato passage. There is not one bar from beginning to end that does not contain the part of one or more instruments. I am assured by the most competent authority that it would be possible to write in the missing parts, and complete the work as Schubert would have done it.

Mr. Sullivan has played it through to me on the piano, and I am allowed by him to say that in quality it appears to be inferior to none of its predecessors, and to abound in beauties;

which I do, earnestly trusting that some means may before long be found of restoring this lost treasure to the world. I have heard that Mendelssohn had at one time the intention of filling it up, but of this I know nothing certain."

These words were written more than ten years ago, but the wish expressed by Mr. Grove has not yet been fulfilled; it is quite likely that Mendelssohn would have filled up the interstices in the symphony had not death removed him so soon after he had acquired it. Mendelssohn is gone from us, but surely there are still musicians who would approach such a task with reverent pleasure, and in whom we should place implicit confidence. To name but one, and perhaps the fittest of them all, Johannes Brahms might be trusted to carry out the work in a manner calculated to satisfy the most enlightened and exacting Schubert admirers.

It should be remembered that here is no question of tampering with the score of a great master, or of presenting his music in a manner contrary to his expressed intentions. Nor is the case similar to that of the unfinished violin concerto of Beethoven recently given to the world, in which Herr Hellmesberger had actually to *compose* in order to bring the movement to a proper conclusion.

Here the entire plan and extent of each section of the work are indicated in the clearest manner, so that doubt is impossible; and as the names of the instruments are given, that *bête noire* of many conscientious musicians — "additional accompaniments" — would not have to be considered.

Another symphony by Schubert! — and one not the product of his boyhood, valuable only as a curiosity, but conceived in his early maturity, only a few months before that other unfinished symphony (No. 8) which is now the delight of all who have ears to hear. The idea fills the mind of the musician with longing which ought to be satisfied.

It only remains to give a synopsis of the several movements of this work. They are as follows:

Adagio in E minor, 4/4 time, 34 bars;

Allegro in E major, 374 bars;

Andante in A, 6/8 time, 116 bars;

Scherzo in C, 3/4 time, 136 bars, with trio in A, 70 bars;

Finale Allegro giusto in E, 2/4 time, 626 bars.

In the course of 1821 Harold's opera *La Clochette* was produced at the Kärnthnerthor Theatre, and Schubert was commissioned to write the two additional numbers for the work mentioned in the catalogue. His name did not appear in connection with the performance, and the pieces were very favourably received, especially the duet.

It will have been noticed that the most uneventful years in Schubert's life were those in which he applied himself most diligently to composition.

Such was 1822, a period which seems to have passed without the occurrence of any incident liable to affect his position to any important extent. But it gave birth to some of his very finest creations.

Meanwhile the publication of his music continued; fourteen songs and part-songs, the First Waltzes (Op.9, D365), and the *Variations on a French Air* (Op.10, D624), seeing the light. The last-named piece is dedicated to Beethoven; and Schindler, in his biography of that great master, relates a very improbable story to the effect that Schubert, with his publisher Diabelli, went in person to present the work to Beethoven, and that his nervousness during the interview was such that he could give no answers to queries addressed to him; his discomfiture being complete when Beethoven pointed out some trifling error in the harmony.

Josef Hüttenbrenner however, states that Beethoven was not at home when Schubert called upon him, and that the two musicians never met, although they lived close to each other for seven years.

There can be little question that Schubert would have stood a better chance of general recognition but for the absorbing influence of his greatest rival. Not that Beethoven was at that time understood by the majority of the musical public; but he was the object of hero worship among the elite.

Schubert's own feelings were, and always had been, those of profound respect and adoration of Beethoven; his instinct enabled him to comprehend the genius of the Bonn master, and the thought of measuring himself against such a giant probably never entered his head.

On his part, Beethoven is said to have been much pleased with the *Variations on a French Air*, but he was too preoccupied to pay much attention to the modest and retiring Schubert. On his death bed, however, a collection of Schubert's songs was placed in his hands, and he expressed the utmost admiration and astonishment at their beauty, exclaiming:

"Truly Schubert possesses a spark of the divine fire ... some day he will make a noise in the world."

The prophecy of the dying man has been amply fulfilled.

As Schubert's songs sold rapidly, he would now have been in comfortable financial circumstances if it were not for his utter helplessness in business matters. His friends did everything that was possible in his interests, but they could not fight all of his battles, and on one unfortunate occasion, when no one was at his elbow, he parted with the copyright of a number of compositions for 800 florins. Among these were the *Erl King* and *The Wanderer*.

Josef Hüttenbrenner made serious efforts to get *Des Teufels Lustschloss* performed in Vienna, Munich, and Prague, but without success. He also applied to the celebrated publishing firm of Peters in Leipsic, and the head of the house replied in a long letter setting forth the difficulties in the way of accepting a new composer's work, but consenting to receive a consignment of pieces. However, for some reason the negotiations came to nothing for a some time.

Around this time, Schubert was offered the position of court organist at Vienna, but he refused it, probably because it would have fettered his actions, confining him to a limited sphere, and he felt that absolute freedom and independence were essential to him.

It is now time to consider what he had accomplished in the way of composition this year.

First, there was the completion of the opera *Alfonso and Estrella*, with the exception of the overture, which was not written until December 1823. It may be readily imagined that Schober's libretto was not a dramatic masterpiece, and the lack of success of the work is doubtless due to that. The subject is wholly romantic, and reflects the warmth and glowing fancy of ardent youth, but the poem is lyrical rather than dramatic. Although this treatment enabled Schubert to pour forth his seemingly inexhaustible stream of melody, it rendered the work unsuitable for stage representation.

It is said that as quickly as Schober wrote his lines, Schubert set them to music, and the librettist expressed his astonishment at this unique display of productive power.

We may share that feeling, though it is impossible to deny that the method adopted by the composer was not likely to end in the production of an effective opera. All sense of dramatic unity and consistency must necessarily have been sacrificed, and instead of an organic whole, the joint efforts of the two friends resulted in a conglomeration of pieces, each one perhaps meritorious and beautiful in itself, but without significance as part of a larger work.

This lack of dramatic power on the part of both poet and musician proved fatal to the chances of *Alfonso and Estrella*, and Schubert did not live to witness a performance of the work. Efforts were made from time to time after his death to arrange for its production, but they were unsuccessful until 1854, when it was performed at Weimar, with the invaluable co-operation of Franz Liszt.

Accounts agree as to the merit of the performance, but not even under such favourable circumstances could its defects be hidden, and the opera was performed only once. The *Neue Zeitschrift für Musik* criticised *Alfonso and Estrella*:

"Unfortunately the poetical, large-hearted composer found himself in company with a thoroughly prosy librettist; for this reason Schubert's opera will have no vitality in it.

The meagre way in which the subject is handled, destitute of any kind of interest, offering no exciting situations, no good dramatic effects, must necessarily have a tame, depressing effect on the audience, not to mention the lyrical effusions which are immoderately dragged out. These last are the peculiar features of this opera (which one might correctly designate a song opera).

The consequence is that Schubert, with his pure vein of melody, must have felt a constant sense of restraint, and cannot get beyond the simplest phrases and forms of his Lieder. The inevitable consequence is a kind of suicidal monotony which Schubert could never succeed, even with his wealth of melody, in entirely dispelling.

This is all the more lamentable, as the composer at any point of the story, where he could rely on support, (for instance at the conclusion of the first act, the first interview of Estrella with Alfonso, with its interesting instrumentation; in the conspirators' chorus at the conclusion of the second act, besides the scene in the third act between Estrella and Adolfo; the march of victory, and much besides,) has given convincing proof of his great powers of operatic writing — had the compiler of the text but held out to the musician a helping hand."

There is here an evident desire to exalt Schubert even at the expense of Schober. Kreissle speaks in detail of the music, his verdict being essentially the same; namely, that where the librettist has afforded an opportunity for dramatic musical treatment, Schubert has not been slow to take advantage of it.

As the score is not available for examination (the original manuscript is in the possession of the Musikfreunde at Vienna), it is impossible to argue against these views; but in view of his published operatic works, it would be wisest to abstain from attempting to prove the universality of Schubert's genius. He did more than enough to earn a place among the great musicians a matter of certainty for all time, and with this knowledge his most fervent admirers may well rest content.

The only portions of *Alfonso and Estrella* which are published are the overture, a cavatina for tenor, *Wenn ich, dich, Holde sehe*, and an aria for bass, *Tief im Getümmel der Schlacht*.

Next in dimensions, and superior in importance, is the Mass in A♭. The score of this work shows that it was composed between November 1819 and September 1822. This unusually long period is not accounted for by any special amount of elaboration in the construction of the work, and an examination of the music tends to prove that the *Kyrie* and *Gloria* were written at the earlier period, and the work then laid aside.

It does not seem to have originated with a view to performance at any particular time; at any rate, there is no mention of such an event, either in Schubert's own correspondence, or in that of his friends. In length, the Mass in Ab stands next to the great work in Eb, the crowning effort of Schubert in church composition. In musical value, it must be placed third among his masses; superior, that is, to those in G, Bb, and C, but inferior to the Eb, and also to the one in F, that marvellous creation of youthful genius. It remained in manuscript until 1875, when it was published in full score.

But the most interesting of Schubert's writings this year, and in some respects the most interesting of all his works, is the Unfinished Symphony in B minor. This, unlike the sketch of the Symphony in E already discussed, is complete as regards the first and second movements.

There are nine bars of the scherzo fully scored, and here the manuscript stops short without the slightest indication of what was to come next. Whether Schubert made a sketch of this movement before commencing to score is not known, not a trace of anything of the kind having come to light.

Perhaps the most curious feature in the case is that he subsequently presented the score, unfinished as it was, to the Musikverein at Gratz, as thanks for the honour conferred upon him by the society electing him as one of its members.

For a long while the work remained in the possession of Anselm Hüttenbrenner, brother of Josef, from where it seems to have passed, according to Nottebohm, into the possession of Johann Herbeck, of Vienna.

It was performed for the first time at one of the Gesellschaft concerts in Vienna, published early in 1867, and introduced into England at a Crystal Palace concert on April 7th in that year. Its subsequent history in this country is too well known to justify the insertion of any further details here, and for the same reason any remarks on its merits would seem like an impertinence.

Symphony no. 8 in B minor ('Unfinished')

Many musicians regard the Unfinished Symphony as Schubert's most individual creation. It seems to be a kind of parable of the composer's own life, a representation in sound of a brief but glorious career abruptly cut short just when its promises were being fulfilled; cut asunder by an inexplicable decree of fate just as the world had begun to understand the beauty and significance of the music.

The passages of great melodic beauty, generally leading with some startling transition into sections of a wild and agitated nature, illustrate faithfully the gleams of happiness which occasionally shot across Schubert's path, only to be followed by a renewal of darkness and failure.

Whether this music conveys a true picture of Schubert's mind, either consciously or unconsciously, no one can say; critics, acting under a natural and understandable impulse, have endeavoured to make such a connection, but apart from one stray sentence in Schubert's diary, as we shall see further on, there is no evidence to prove that he sought to depict his own feelings in his music.

The year 1823 brought with it one or two matters of considerable importance to Schubert, and it was also an active period in terms of composition.

In October of this year Weber's *Euryanthe* was produced in Vienna, the composer having come to that city for the express purpose of conducting his new opera. It would be pleasant to be able to report a friendly meeting between two musicians so thoroughly imbued with German feeling, and who for that reason should have felt sympathy and admiration for each other's aims and aspirations.

The possibility of such a natural bond of union did not, however, prevent Schubert from criticising with severity the obvious defects of *Euryanthe* — defects which were more the fault of Helmina Chezy, the librettist, than of Carl Maria von Weber, the musician. His assertion that *Euryanthe* contained

not one original melody, and very little genius, went far beyond the mark, and Weber no doubt felt justified in his angry retort to the effect that "the blockhead should learn something first before he presumes to judge me."

Schubert, unabashed, took the score of his *Alfonso and Estrella* to Weber to prove that he had already learned something, The composer of *Der Freischütz* looked through the score, and then remarked that it was the usual course to "drown the first puppies and burn the first operas."

Of course he only shared the general ignorance as to the marvellous extent and value of Schubert's productions. It is said that Weber's unfriendly expressions arose entirely from pique at Schubert's harsh criticism of his own work, and that subsequently he spoke highly of *Alfonso and Estrella*, and was willing to have it performed at the Dresden Opera, of which he was then conductor. But it is certain that these two men did not regard each other with the cordiality which one might have hoped for under the circumstances.

The eccentric, and indeed half-crazy, authoress Helmina von Chezy, who had been the means of causing the gifted and popular Weber to fail in his new opera, was now about to weigh down the genius of Franz Schubert in a similar manner. This arose under somewhat peculiar circumstances.

A beautiful actress in Vienna, Fraülein Neumann, had an admirer named Kupelwieser, who was acquainted with Madame Chezy. He asked her to write a drama to which Schubert was to supply incidental music, all this for the benefit of his young actress at the Theater an der Wien.

Madame Chezy undertook the task, and finished it in five days, though convinced, as she says, of the unsuitability of her work for this particular theatre, whose public had a preference for pieces of a realistic and highly coloured description; picturesque melodramas and broad extravaganzas. Further, the director of the house, Wilhelm Vogel, had written a piece, *Der böse Krollo*, purposely for the benefit of Fraülein Neumann, and in a style more suited to his patrons.

However Schubert accepted his part of the task, and the performance took place on December 20th. The piece was described in the bill:

> "*Rosamunde, Princess of Cyprus.* Romantic play in four acts, with choruses, musical accompaniments and dances, by Helmina Chezy *née* Klencke. Music by Herr Schubert."

Accounts are unanimous as to the heaviness, monotony, and obscurity of the drama, but the music was very warmly received, thanks in part to Schubert's friends, who attended in force, and applauded vociferously. The overture was that to *Alfonso and Estrella*, then just composed.

A critic in the periodical *Der Sammler* described the music:

> "Herr Schubert shows originality in his compositions, but unfortunately *bizarrerie* also. The young man is in a period of development; we hope that he will come out of it successfully. At present he is too much applauded; for the future, may he never complain of being too little recognised."

Had the writer for *Der Sammler* been permitted to see the future, his astonishment at Schubert's place in music would have been immense. *Rosamunde* was performed just twice, and then laid aside in favour of Vogel's *Der böse Krollo*. In 1824, the romance and the three choruses were published with piano accompaniment.

In 1828, the overture to *Die Zauberharfe* was published in a four-hand arrangement as the overture to *Rosamunde*, and this title it has since preserved. The orchestral parts to the romance and choruses, as well as the pretty shepherd's melody and a third *entracte*, were discovered by Mr. Greorge Grove in a cupboard at Dr. Schneider's, where they had lain undisturbed for 44 years.

The next important dramatic work composed this year was the opera *Fierabras*. Barbaja, the manager of the Imperial Opera, had commissioned Josef Kupelwieser, the secretary of the Josefstadt Theatre, to write the libretto, and Schubert composed the whole of the music to three acts between May 25th and October 2nd. According to the dates on the score, the first act, consisting of 300 pages, was written in five days. It was so much labour wasted, however, as Barbaja's lease of the theatre came shortly to an end; and *Fierabras* was not accepted for performance by his successor.

The opera is set in Spain, and the story is purely romantic, dealing with the wars with the Moors. According to Kreissle's description, the action seems well sustained, with plenty of

A Schubertiade

heroic and sentimental excitement.

The music consists of the overture and 22 numbers. As the opera has not yet been published in its complete form, it is impossible to judge its merits, the only portions at present available being the overture, a soprano air with male chorus (*Des Jammers herbe Qualen*), and a chorus of Moors (*Der Rache Opfer fallen*).

Fierabras has never been performed in public. If we may form an opinion from mere description, it might be better suited for stage representation today than any other of Schubert's dramatic works. Whether this is so or not, the world should not be deprived of this music, written in the composer's prime, and doubtless abounding in beauties.

This did not conclude his labours for the theatre this year. Among the writers of light and ephemeral pieces, mostly adapted from the French, was I. F. Castelli, who published about this time a one act libretto, *Die Verschworenen*. The author's preface is worth quoting:

"The general complaint of German composers is this:

'We should be very pleased to write operas if we could obtain suitable poems!'

Now here is one, gentlemen! If you will set it to music, please let my words have fair play, and don't spoil the plot, whilst you only look after roulades and flourishes in preference to musical characteristics.

In my opinion, the opera should be a dramatically worked piece, accompanied with music — not music with a text adapted as an afterthought; and the general effect and impression, according to my view, are of more importance than that of giving an opportunity for some individual singer to display the elasticity and power of his voice. Let us do something, gentlemen, for German opera!"

The soundness of the views expressed above is undeniable. Schubert must have seized upon the piece immediately after its publication, for the date at the end of his score is April 1823; there is no date at the commencement.

Castelli and Schubert were acquainted with each other, but the composer, with characteristic carelessness, never even mentioned to the librettist that he had set *Die Verschworenen*. However, both he and Josef Hüttenbrenner made serious efforts to get the work performed, but without success. A diary entry from 1824 states:

"*Der häusliche Krieg* [the title subsequently given to the operetta], written at my father's house, reviewed and passed for performance at the Royal Opera House."

On the other hand; when the piece was produced at Munich in 1862, the *Augsburg Zeitung*, in its notice, stated that

> "A year after Schubert had given his opera to the managers of the Opera House, he thought the time had arrived for him to make some inquiries as to the fate of his work. Whereupon he got back his score from the library, rolled up, tied, and fastened — in short, in exactly the same state as he had sent it thirteen months before, to his wise judges and reviewers."

This story has never been corroborated.

The plot of *Der häusliche Krieg* is an adaptation of Aristophanes' *Lysistrata*. Its humour is rather broad and unrefined, but the treatment shows a good knowledge of stage effect, and offers plenty of scope for piquant musical treatment.

But Schubert could not abandon himself thoroughly to the exigencies of dramatic representation. He was at all times intensely subjective as a composer, and did not perceive the necessity of subjugating, or even controlling, his lyrical impulses for the better realisation of the various situations in an operatic framework.

Thus we find in *Der häusliche Krieg*, as in his earlier dramatic works, a lavish quantity of delicious melody, whenever an opportunity offers itself.

But of the true dramatic instinct there is but little to be found, and as *Der häusliche Krieg* was the last of his completed works for the stage, we must say that as an operatic composer, Schubert missed his mark. His very inventiveness was a stumbling block to him.

But in the concert room, the music of his lyric dramas will always be welcome. *Der häusliche Krieg* remained unknown till 1861, when it was performed at a concert of the Vienna Musikverein, and created a most favourable impression.

In August of the same year it was performed in Frankfurt, and performances in several other German cities followed quickly. The score was published by Spina in 1862. On March 2, 1872, the opera was performed at a Crystal Palace concert.

The most interesting and valuable of his compositions in 1823 is the charming cycle of songs known as *Die schöne Müllerin*. The circumstances surrounding the production of this lovely work show the composer in a characteristic light.

One day he called upon Herr Randhartinger, secretary to Count Seczenyi, and was asked to wait a short time. Taking up a volume of Müller's poems, he read a few lines, and then put the book in his pocket and went away. Next day the secretary went to Schubert for his book, and was presented with No. 1 of the *Müllerlieder*.

Fourteen other songs were written this year, several of his greatest favourites being among them. The well known song *Der Zwerg* was composed in the shop of the music publishers, Sauer and Leidesdorf, Schubert maintaining at the same time an animated conversation with a friend.

The extraordinary speed with which he wrote and his ability

to compose in every kind of unfavourable circumstance suggested the idea to his friend, Johann Vogl, that he wrote whilst in a state of clairvoyance.

This theory was supported by the following incident.

Among some songs recently composed was one to which Vogl took a special fancy, but finding it too high for him, he had a copy written in a lower key. A fortnight later he performed the song in Schubert's presence, and the composer exclaimed "Hm! A pretty good song. Who wrote it?"

Taking into consideration not only the multitude of his compositions, but also his careless treatment of them, this forgetfulness of one of his own songs was not so very surprising.

One of the finest of the instrumental works this year is the piano Sonata in A minor (D784), the slow movement of which is worthy of Beethoven for breadth and grandeur. Reissmann places this work as far back as 1817, but an examination of the music is sufficient to prove this date erroneous. Among the publications in 1823 were the piano Fantasia in C, a set of dances, six male voice part songs, and seventeen Lieder.

Of Schubert's personal movements at this time very little is known. He spent the whole year in Vienna, living for the most part in his father's house, according to the memoranda on his compositions, and subsisting of course on the sale of these.

Portrait of Schubert by Melegh Gabor, 1827.
Hungarian National Gallery, Budapest.

SCHUBERT.   1500

6

Schubert's temporary depression — Diary and letters — Second visit to Zelész and love for Caroline Esterhazy — Compositions; the duet sonata in C — Travels in Steyr — Restored cheerfulness — Efforts to gain a position — Negotiations with foreign publishers — Present from the Musikfreunde — Beethoven's funeral — Visit to the Pachlers at Gratz — Failing health — Rochlitz and Der Erste Ton.

W E NOW APPROACH a period in Schubert's life when the clouds of destiny were gathering around him. Repeated disappointments, a monotonous existence and bodily weakness all contributed to produce a state of mental depression.

The unhappy frequently find some consolation in writing down their thoughts, and Schubert kept a diary at this time, from which Kreissle has made the following extracts:

> "Grief sharpens the understanding and strengthens the soul, whereas joy seldom troubles itself about the former, and makes the latter either effeminate or frivolous."

> "March 27th — No one fathoms another's grief, no one another's joy. People think they are ever going *to* one another, and they only go *near* one another. Oh, the misery of he who knows this by experience!"

"My productions in music that are the product of understanding, and spring from my sorrow, those only which are the product of pain, seem to please the world the most. The loftiest inspiration is but a step removed from the absolutely ludicrous, just as the deepest wisdom is so near akin to crass stupidity.

With faith man steps forth into the world. Faith is far ahead of understanding and knowledge; for to understand anything, I must first of all believe something. Faith is the higher basis on which weak understanding rears its first columns of proof; reason is nothing but faith analysed."

"March 29. — Oh Fancy! Thou unsearchable fountain at which artists and philosophers quench their thirst! Oh, stay with us, although known and honoured but by few; stay with us, if only to guard us against so-called enlightenment, that skeleton without flesh and blood."

On March 31st, Schubert wrote the following to Professor Leopold Kupelwieser, brother of Josef, who wrote the libretto of *Fierabras* and arranged the production of *Rosamunde*. Herein his inmost feelings are portrayed in vivid colours:

"Dear Kupelwieser, I have been anxious for some time past to write to you, but I didn't know how to manage it. An opportunity however is now offered me, and at last I can once more pour out my heart to somebody. You are so good, so honest and true, you will surely forgive me much which others would take offence at.

In one word I feel myself the most unhappy, the most miserable man on earth. Picture to yourself a man whose health can never be re-established, who from sheer despair makes matters worse instead of better; picture to yourself, I say, a man whose most brilliant hopes have come to nothing, to whom the happiness of proffered love and friendship is but anguish, whose enthusiasm for the beautiful (an inspired feeling at least) threatens to vanish altogether— and then ask yourself if such a condition does not represent a miserable and unhappy man?

'Meine Ruh ist hin, mein Herz ist schwer,
Ich finde sie nimmer und nimmermehr.'

I can repeat these lines now every day; for every night when I go to sleep I hope never to awake, and every morning renews afresh the wounds of yesterday.

Friendless, joylessly should I drag on the days of my existence were it not that sometimes my brain reels, and a gleam of the sweet days that are gone shoots across my vision.

Our society, as you will have known by this time, came to an end from the reinforcement of the coarse crew addicted to beer drinking and sausage eating; its dissolution followed in two days, although I gave up attending immediately after your departure.

Leidesdorf,[1] with whom I am intimately acquainted, is a thoroughly sound, good man, but so deeply depressed and melancholy that I fear I have gained from him more than is

---

[1] The music publisher.

good for me in this respect. Then, both his and my affairs are not prosperous, and consequently we never have money.

Your brother's opera (I don't admire his conduct in absenting himself from the theatre) was declared impracticable, and no demand of any sort was made for my music.

Castelli's opera *Die Verschworenen*[1] has been received with applause at Berlin: the music is by a resident composer there. Thus I have composed two operas to no purpose whatever. I have done very little new in the way of songs; but, to make amends, I have made several attempts in instrumental things, for I have composed two quartets, besides an octet, and I intend to write an additional quartet; thus I hope to pave the way for a grand symphony.

The latest news in Vienna is that Beethoven intends giving a concert, when we are to have his new symphony, three numbers out of the new mass, and a new overture. God willing, I intend also to give a similar concert next year. Now I conclude, not wishing to use too much letter paper, and greet you a thousand times.

If you were to write all about your artistic and intellectual state just at present, and your life generally, nothing would give greater pleasure to your true friend,

Franz Schubert

P.S. My address would be, 'An die Kunsthandlung Sauer, and Leidesdorf, because at the beginning of March, I go with Esterhazy to Hungary."

---

[1] A more fortunate setting of the same libretto.

These extracts are indicative of a morbid frame of mind. But it would be grossly unjust to quote them, as some have done, to prove that Schubert's normal condition was unhappy, and that he regarded himself as the victim of a relentless fate, ever dooming him to failure and disappointment. His natural disposition was to take matters easily and unconcernedly, and this outburst of complaining was only the result of one of those temporary fits of depression to which most men are subject at some period of their lives.

Also, it would be deceptive to gauge the state of his mind from the character of his music: in the midst of this mental gloom he composed the octet for strings and wind, one of the most uniformly cheerful of his works.

In the letter quoted above, he mentions that he is going to the Esterhazys at Zelész. Six years had elapsed since he was last there, and there is nothing to suggest that the arrangement made in 1818 was not followed up annually.

Nor is there any evidence that he even continued to teach the family or maintain his relationship with them during their winter residence in Vienna. But, from a certain incident now to be narrated, it is probable that the connection was not sundered for so long a period as six years.

It may seem surprising that up to the present time no mention has been made of any affair of the heart in which Schubert was concerned. One in whom the poetic and imaginative qualities were so richly developed might be thought to have been susceptible to passion. However, this was not so, even though he was fond of rallying his friends on their various flirtations.

After the failure of his relationship with Therese Grob, only once in his entire life did he again show strong feelings for a woman; Caroline Esterhazy, the younger daughter of Count Esterhazy. Kreissle refers to the matter on the occasion of Schubert's first visit to Zelész in 1818. But Caroline was then

Caroline Esterhazy

Mártha Eggerth as Caroline Esterhazy in the
1934 film *Unfinished Symphony*.

a girl of eleven, and he was 21. It is probable therefore that the affair commenced at a later date, and it is certain that it culminated in 1824.

Caroline was now seventeen years old, and her increasing beauty and attractive manners apparently enslaved her music teacher. That she was aware of his passion cannot be doubted, and one day she asked him, with pretended feelings of earnestness, why he never dedicated any of his pieces to her. He replied:

> "What would be the use? All that I do
> is dedicated to you."

But although she admired and liked him, as did the rest of her family, she could not return his love; and, considering the disparity in their ages and positions, and Schubert's ordinary appearance, there is no cause for wonder at this.

Romanticists will delight in connecting the state of his heart with the music he composed about this time. This biographer cannot deal with such conjectures, but will now pass on to the more practical question of the influence of a trip to Hungary on Schubert's imagination.

With all his subjectivity, he could not have been impervious to everything that is fascinating in Slavonic music, and we find an unmistakable Hungarian influence in several compositions from the year 1824.

The *Divertissement à la Hongroise* for four hands (D818), is one of these; and the Quartet in A minor (D804), a work of far greater beauty and value, is another. The two Quartets in E♭ (D87) and E (D353), were written this year, though previous to his visit to Zelész (according to his letter to Kupelwieser); but the Variations (D813), are dated from that place, and so is the magnificent Sonata in C for four hands (D812). This splendid work was composed in June, according to the manuscript in the possession of Madame Schumann.

Its eminently orchestral character is obvious to all musicians, and Herr Joachim, recognising this, has scored it in the most tasteful and appropriate manner. Of course he has thereby incurred the displeasure of the pedants, which in this instance he can well afford to disregard.

In the letter to Kupelwieser, Schubert speaks of writing a grand symphony. No such work saw the light until 1828. Might not this be the symphony, disguised thus, because no orchestra was available at Zelész? It is permissible to think so, and, having regard to the character of the work, Herr Joachim should receive the gratitude of all Schubert's admirers for having recognized one of Schubert's most valuable bequests.

The Sonata in A Minor for piano and harp mentioned by Kreissle is probably actually that for piano and arpeggione.

Among the vocal compositions there is the celebrated quartet *Gebet vor der Schacht*. The composition of this piece provided the Esterhazys with an example of Schubert's extraordinary capacity.

One morning, at breakfast, the Countess begged him to set

De la Motte Fouqué's poem to music. That evening he presented the quartet, and it was practised at once. The manuscript remained in the possession of the Countess until 1838, when it was published.

The change of scene and occupation had an ameliorating influence on Schubert's mind, as will be seen by the following extracts from a serious, but on the whole cheerful, letter to his brother Ferdinand:

> "Was it merely sorrow at my absence that drew tears from you, which you could not trust yourself to write about? Or on thinking of me, oppressed as I am by indefinable longings, did you feel yourself enveloped in a gloomy veil of sorrow? Or did all the tears which you have already seen me shed come to your remembrance?
>
> For, come what may, I feel more plainly than ever at this moment that you, and no one else, are my own precious friend, interwoven with every fibre of my soul. In order that these lines may not perchance mislead you to a belief that I am unwell or out of spirits, I hasten to assure you of the contrary.
>
> Certainly that happy joyous time is gone, when every object seemed encircled with a halo of youthful glory; and that which has followed is a miserable reality, which I endeavour, as far as possible, to embellish by the gifts of my fancy (for which I thank God) ...
>
> I am now, much more than formerly, finding peace and happiness in myself. As a proof of this I shall show you a grand sonata and variations upon an original theme, which I have already composed."

This letter is dated July 18th. The picture it draws of the tone poet finding consolation for the disappointments of life in the exercise of his art shows that Schubert was beginning, instinctively, to comprehend his mission in the world.

The publications of 1824 comprise the *Müllerlieder*, dedicated to the Baron von Schönstein, the friend of the Esterhazys, the vocal pieces from *Rosamunde*, the three marches for four hands (D602), and the part song, *Der Gondelfahrer*.

Next year the clouds drifted away from Schubert, and he became once more buoyant, jovial, and mirth-loving. This change for the better was brought about by a long excursion which he took with Vogl in the region of Upper Austria.

The friends met at Steyr on March 31st, where they remained until the warm weather set in, enjoying the hospitality of their many friends, and rewarding them with their musical performances. In their subsequent wanderings they also fell in constantly with old acquaintances, whose companionship greatly added to the delights of travel in a beautiful country.

Schubert's feelings at this time can be understood by allowing him to speak for himself. Here is part of a letter written to his old schoolfriend, Joseph Spaun:

"Linz, July 21, 1825.

Dear Spaun, You may well imagine my uncommon vexation in being obliged in Linz to write a letter to you in Lemberg.[1] Deuce take that abominable duty which separates friends from one another when they had scarce sipped the cup of friendship!

Here I am sitting still in Linz, half dead with the melting heat and perspiration. I have a whole number of new songs, and you are not

---

[1] He expected to have met his friend in Linz, but business had called Spaun away before his arrival.

here. Are you not ashamed? Linz without you is a body without a soul, a rider without a horse, broth without salt. If I didn't get good beer at Jagermaier's, and decent wine at the Schlossberg, I should go and hang myself on the parade out of grief for the soul of the Linzers, which has taken wing and flown away.

You see, I am utterly out of sorts with the general lot of Linz folk, whereas in your mother's house, surrounded by your sisters, besides Attenwalt, and Max, I am thoroughly happy: a faint shadow of their spirit seems to radiate from the material form of an occasional Linzer. Only I fear this light will become less beautiful by degrees, and then I shall fall to pieces in sheer despair.

After all it is downright misery to see everything ossified into stale prose, whilst the majority of humdrum people jog on in perfect self-complacency, as long as they can comfortably slide over the quagmire into the abyss below. It certainly is much harder work as one mounts upward in the scale, and yet it would be an easy matter to get rid of the common elements, if the upper classes lent a helping hand.

For the rest, don't let your hair grow grey with misery at being so far away from us. Brave the simple fate; let your gentle spirit expand like a flower garden, that you may diffuse the warmth of life in the cold north, and show your divine origin wherever you go. Contemptible is the grief which stealthily creeps upon a noble heart; cast it away from you, and tear to pieces the vulture which is gnawing at your soul."

Schubert's genial nature shows himself here unmistakably. On July 25th he sent a long letter to his parents, from which a few brief extracts are presented:

> "My new songs out of Walter Scott's *Lady of the Lake* were very warmly commended. My audience expressed great delight at the solemnity of my *Hymn to the Blessed Virgin*; it seems to instill in the minds of listeners a spirit of piety and devotion. I believe I have attained this result by never forcing on myself religious ecstasy, and never setting myself to compose such hymns or prayers, except when I am involuntarily overcome by the feeling and spirit of devotion; in that case devotion is of the right and genuine kind .....
>
> I intend to have some other arrangement for the publication of these songs, the present one inviting so little attention. They must have the illustrious name of Scott on the title page, and thus make people more curious: with the addition of the English text, they might help to make me better known in England, if only once I could but make some fair terms with publishers; but in that matter the wise and beneficent management of the Government has taken care that the artist shall remain forever the slave of every huckster.
>
> With regard to Milder's letter, I am glad to hear of the favourable reception given to Zuleika, although I should have liked to have examined the review for myself to see if there was anything to be learned from it; for however favourable the criticism may be, the whole thing may be simply ridiculous, if the reviewer, as is often the case, has not the

proper understanding and capacity for reviewing ...

Give my kindest love to Ferdinand and his wife and children ... If only he could see these divine mountains and lakes, the look of which threatens to crush or to swallow us, he would not be so enamoured of the petty life of men as not to esteem it a great happiness to be restored anew to life and strength and energy.

What of Carl? Will he travel, or stay at home? He has now a great deal to do; for a married artist is bound to publish pieces from nature, as well as copies; and if both kinds succeed, he is doubly to be praised, for that is no light matter to attain unto. I renounce it on that account..."

These are not the utterances of a man who is thoroughly tired and disgusted with existence, and whose mind has become unhinged by long-continued striving with unkind fortune. The simple piety and sly humour are characteristic of Schubert at his best; and the shrewdness in business matters shows that he was beginning, at least, to acquire a little knowledge of the world.

Later in the season he sent Ferdinand a detailed account of his wanderings, from which we now quote a few passages. The first portion is dated Gmunden, September 12th:

"From Neumarkt, which is the last stage before Salzburg, one gets the first glimpse of the snow-covered tops of mountains emerging from the Salzburg valley. About an hour from Neumarkt the country is exceedingly beautiful. The Waller See, which pours forth its clear bluish-greenish water, lights up this fair scene in an enchanting way. The situation is very lofty, and from that point one gets by a constant descent as far as Salzburg. The mountains appear higher and higher; the Untersberg, with its ghosts and legends, peers above the rest like magic. The villages show signs of the wealth of former days.

In the commonest peasants' houses, one finds marble window ledges and doors, sometimes even staircases of red marble. The sun darkens and the gloomy clouds lower over the black mountains like children of the mist; but they touch not the peak of the Untersburg; they glide past it as though afraid of its dreadful inmates ...

From the Cathedral we went to the Monastery of St. Peter, where Michael Haydn resided. The church here also is wonderfully beautiful. Here, as you know, is the monument of Haydn. It is very fine, but is badly placed in an obscure, out-of-the-way corner. The inscriptions all about, in different directions, have something childish about them. Haydn's head is contained in an urn.

I thought to myself, 'May thy pure and peaceful spirit hover around me, dear Haydn! And if I can never become like thee, peaceful and guileless, at all events none on earth has such deep reverence for thee as I have.' (Sad tears fell from my eyes and we went on).

~ Steyr, September 21."

"You see from the date that several days have elapsed between this and my last letter, and that from Gmunden we have, alas, settled down again at Steyr. To continue, then, the diary of my journey (which I already repent of — it takes me too long):

The following day was the loveliest day in the world, and of the world. The Untersberg, or more properly the Oberste, shone and glistened amidst his squadron and attendant crowd of other mountains in, or strictly speaking near, the sun.

We drove through the above-described valley, and thought ourselves in Elysium, with this advantage over the paradise of old: that we sat in a charming carriage — a luxury unknown to Adam and Eve. Instead of wild beasts, all sorts of pretty girls met us on our way.

It really is very wrong that in so lovely a country I should make such sorry jokes, but today I can't be serious for a single moment ....

After some hours we arrived at Hallein, a remarkable town, but uncommonly dirty and dismal. All the inhabitants look like ghosts, pale, hollow-eyed, and thin enough to make tapers of, or lucifer matches. The horrible contrast suggested by a comparison of the Ratzenstadtl with the other valley made a strong impression on my mind. It is as though one fell straight from heaven upon a dungheap ... and amidst these awful scenes man has sought to perpetuate the memory of his still even more dreadful inhuman actions.

For here it was that the Bavarians on one side of the Salzach, and the Tyrolese on the other, the river roaring deep beneath them, inflicted that dreadful, murderous slaughter on each other. Here it was that the Tyrolese, secreted among the rocks, uttering their hellish cries, fired on the Bavarians, who were striving to take the pass, and fell wounded into the abyss.

This shameful action, which continued for several days and weeks, was commemorated by building a chapel on the Bavarian side of the pass, and erecting a red cross in the rock on the Tyrolese side. These emblems were partly intended as memorials, and partly to appease the wrath of Heaven.

Oh, glorious Christ, how many wicked deeds must Thy sacred image appear to sanction! Thou, Thyself, the cruellest memorial of human guilt; men set up Thy image as though they would say: 'Lo! with insolent feet, we have trampled upon the most perfect creation of the great God; should we feel disturbed compunction of heart in annihilating that noxious insect called man?'

Schubert and Vogl

Gracious Heaven! It's an awful business having to describe one's travels. I can't say more. As I intend to come to Vienna in the early part of October, I will present you with my diary in person, and where I have omitted anything you shall have it from my lips."

Shortly after this Vogl departed for Italy to be treated for the gout; and as Schubert's money was nearly all spent, he returned to Vienna, light of pocket, but thoroughly restored in body and mind.

If he could have renewed these pleasant excursions at frequent intervals, his life might have been extended by a few years at least. But, with the exception of a brief visit to Gratz in 1827, this was the last occasion on which he left Vienna.

While he was enjoying the beauties of nature in the Austrian Tyrol, and of art in Salzburg, his pen was not idle. The wild and beautiful Sonata in A Minor (D845), was certainly written during his wanderings, and Nottebohm names the Sonatas in D (D850), and in A (D664), as being probably composed this year. Reissmann is undoubtedly wrong in placing these works as early as 1817. They are both in his later manner — the Sonata in D especially.

Publication proceeded this year, the A Minor Quartet (D804), several songs and piano pieces, as far as D209, being included in the catalogue. No record is to be found of the sums received by Schubert for these works, but the honorarium was doubtless in all cases very small, as his finances were in an unsatisfactory state at the end of the year.

Ten years had elapsed since Schubert made his unsuccessful application for the post of music master at Laibach, and since that time he had not tried to obtain any employment. In 1826, however, he made two such moves, failing in the first by mere ill-fortune, and in the second through his own folly, if we are to believe the story.

The office of Vicecapellmeister to the Imperial Court becoming vacant, Schubert applied for the position. Among the other candidates were Ignaz Ritter von Seyfried, Conradin Kreutzer, Anselm Hüttenbrenner, and Josef Weigl. Count Harrach, the Hofmusikgraf, in making his report concerning the merits of the candidates, said of Schubert:

"Schubert appeals to his services as Court singer, confirmed by a testimonial of Salieri, who taught him composition, and vouches for the fact of his having composed five masses, which have been given in several churches."

The decision was not made until January in the following year.

As Schindler is the authority for the details of the other affair; and as there are circumstances in it hard to believe, it would be only just to let him tell the story in his own words:

"Schubert had an opportunity in 1826 of freeing himself from his monetary difficulties by obtaining a respectable appointment. In consequence of Capellmeister Krebs leaving for Hamburg, a conductor was required for the Kärnthnerthor Theatre, and Schubert's friends, with Vogl at their head, tried their utmost to get him appointed.

The young musician had attracted the attention of Duport, the manager; but the decision rested upon his success in composing some operatic scenes arranged for the occasion. This was done, and Nanette Schechner was to sing the soprano part. During the rehearsals, the lady called the attention of the composer to some insurmountable difficulties in the principal air, and asked him to make curtailments and to simplify the accompaniments, which Schubert flatly refused to do.

At the first orchestral rehearsal the artist endeavoured in vain to master the air, and Schubert's friends begged him to make the required modifications, but without result. He persisted in his determination.

At the last rehearsal everything went smoothly until the air, when it happened as everyone anticipated; the singer struggled with the weighty accompaniments, especially with the brass, but she was overpowered. She sat down on a chair by the proscenium, quite exhausted.

No one spoke, and despair was on every face. Meanwhile Duport, the manager, went from group to group and whispered mysteriously. As for Schubert, he sat motionless, during this most unpleasant scene, like a statue, his eyes fixed upon the score lying open in front of him. At length Buport advanced to the orchestra and said, very politely,

'Herr Schubert, we should like to postpone the performance for a few days; and I must request that you will make the requisite alterations in the aria, so as to render it easier for Fraulein Schechner.'

Several members of the orchestra now entreated Schubert to yield; but his anger was only intensified by Duport's observations and these added entreaties, and exclaiming in a loud voice, 'I alter nothing,' he closed the book with a bang, put it under his arm, and strode away quickly.

All hope of his appointment was of course abandoned."

This extraordinary story rests solely on the authority of Schindler, whose untrustworthiness with regard to Beethoven has been often exposed.

That Schubert was averse to altering anything he had written was undoubtedly true. Carl Umlauff, a musical amateur,

relates that he often used to visit him early in the morning, and generally found him in bed noting down his ideas. Umlauff would sing Schubert's newest songs with a guitar accompaniment, sometimes venturing to question the advisability of the expression given to certain words. But Schubert was very tenacious of his own views, and would never agree to alter what had been written down.

On one occasion there was an argument over the line in *The Wanderer*, 'Oh Land, wo bist du?'. Schubert insisted upon emphasising the word 'bist' and Umlauff the word 'du'. Schubert stuck to his opinion, and the line was published in this form.

On the other hand, it is difficult to believe that Schubert, who was rarely known to lose his temper, would behave in the extraordinary manner Schindler has described.

An eye-witness of the rehearsal at the Kärnthnerthor Theatre, Franz Zierer, says that the scene was difficult; but remembers no unpleasantness, asserting, indeed, that Schubert behaved in his usual quiet and undemonstrative manner.

Josef Hüttenbrenner declares that Fräulein Schechner expressed herself delighted "with the beautiful air by Schubert," and that theatrical intrigues were the reason for his failure to win the appointment.

An examination of the piece would probably put an end to all doubt on the subject; but unhappily it has been lost, and, thanks to Schindler, Schubert must still be suspected of having ruined his own prospects through folly.

At the same time, as Kreissle observes, it is not likely that he would have remained at his post even if he had obtained it. His love of change, his independent spirit, and his free, untutored manner would not have agreed with the routine duties of a theatrical conductor.

Meanwhile, his reputation as a composer was gradually spreading, and this year negotiations were carried on with publishers in distant cities regarding the purchase of his works. Probst, of Leipsic, wrote to him, on August 26th, offering to take some Lieder and piano pieces written in a comprehensible style, and free from the composer's usual 'eccentric manner'.

Breitkopf and Härtel, the most celebrated German music publishers, in reply to overtures from Schubert, stated in a letter dated September 7th their willingness to issue one or two piano pieces if Schubert would accept a number of copies in lieu of money. This caution may seem strange and short-sighted to us today, but it was perhaps understandable for a publisher dealing with a man whose name was scarcely known outside his own select circle.

These communications had no practical result in 1826; but in Vienna publication went on apace, even as far as Opus 67 (D734). There is a memorandum in Nottebohm's catalogue that for the Sonata in D, No. 2 (D823), and the *Divertissement à la Hongroise* (D818), Schubert received 300 gulden from Artaria.

As to composition, there was no falling off, either in extent or value, as will be seen by the catalogue.

The two magnificent Quartets in D Minor and G were both written this year, the latter in the ten days from June 20th to 30th. Thanks to the variations on *Der Tod und das Mädchen*, the Quartet in D Minor is the more popular of the two; but the one in G is the finer. They are both glorious compositions, unequalled save by the best creations of Beethoven in the same form.

As Schubert did not travel this year, and his music was published so rapidly, he was probably in a more comfortable financial position at its close. On October 12th he received the following note, together with a purse of 100 gulden, from the Gesellschaft der Musikfreunde:

> "You have given this society repeated proofs of your sympathy and the interest you take in its welfare, and devoted your distinguished talents as a composer to the benefit of this institution, and you have also been a special benefactor to the Conservatorium. The Society, capable of appreciating the full value of your remarkable powers as a composer, wishes to convey to you some appropriate token of its gratitude and esteem, and begs your acceptance of the enclosed present, not as a payment, but an acknowledgement on the part of the Society of the obligations it is under to you, for the zeal and interest you have taken in its welfare.
>
> ~ From the Committee for the Amateur Society of the Austrian Kaiserstadt."

The compositions referred to must be the 23rd Psalm, and *Gott in der Natur*, written for the pupils of the Conservatorium.

Johann Jenger, Anselm Huttenbrenner and Franz Schubert.
Drawing by Josef Teltscher.

Schubert made a rich return for the compliment paid him by the Musikfreunde. He presented them in 1828 with the score of his great Symphony in C; but as will be seen, they did not at the time know how to appreciate the gift.

On January 22nd, 1827, the decision regarding the appointment of Vicecapellmeister was made known. Josef Weigl, composer of *Die Schweizerfamilie* and a large number of works of all types of music, was the fortunate candidate; and thus Schubert again found himself deprived of the chance of obtaining a regular income, as well as an honourable position. When he was informed of Weigl's selection he said to Spaun:

> "I should have been very glad to receive that appointment, but as it has been given to so excellent a musician as Weigl I have no cause for dissatisfaction."

Early this same year, the musical world was startled to learn of the dangerous illness of Beethoven.

Notwithstanding Schindler's description of the great master's reception of Schubert in 1822, there is no direct evidence that the two composers met at that time. Josef Hüttenbrenner, whose testimony may be trusted, states however that he, Schubert, and the artist Teltscher went to Beethoven's house during his last illness, and stood for a long while round his bed. The dying man was told the names of his visitors, and made signs to them with his hand which they could not comprehend. Schubert was deeply touched on this occasion. His veneration for the greatest of all musicians amounted to something resembling worship.

Shortly afterwards the news went out that the mighty Beethoven was dead, and Schubert was among the crowd that attended his funeral. A Viennese journal states that he was one of the 38 torch bearers who stood around the grave.

After the ceremony, he adjourned with two friends to the Mehlgrube tavern, where he filled two glasses of wine, and drank the first to the memory of Beethoven, and the second to the memory of he who would be the first to follow Beethoven to the grave.

People often like to think that everyone is mortal but themselves; Schubert probably little dreamed that he himself would follow Beethoven's in footsteps in less than two years.

Any gloomy considerations were for a while dispelled by a pleasurable excursion which Schubert made late in the summer of this year.

At Gratz there lived a family by the name of Pachler, whose house was a rendezvous for many connected with art, and especially with music. Frau Pachler, the wife of Dr. Carl Pachler, was gifted far above the average with musical ability. She was a devoted admirer of Beethoven, and played his sonatas with great intelligence.

Musicians of note were always sure of a welcome at the Pachler house, and Beethoven himself had been expected in 1827, his death putting an end forever to this hope.

Schubert's friend Johann Jenger was friendly with the family, and had been commissioned to bring him in 1826, but business matters disrupted this arrangement, and it was postponed until next year.

On June 12th, Schubert wrote the following to Frau Pachler:

> "Most gracious Lady, — Although I am at a loss to account for my deserving at your hands the friendly invitation forwarded me in a letter sent to Jenger, and without ever supposing it will be in my power to make any kind of return for your goodness, yet I cannot but accept an invitation which will not only enable me to see Gratz, the praises of which place have become so familiar to me, but also to have the honour of becoming personally acquainted with you.
>
> I remain, with every sentiment of respect, your most obedient servant,
> Franz Schubert."

The guests arrived at Gratz on Monday, September 3rd, and had a very pleasant time of it for nearly three weeks. Excursions to places of interest in the neighbourhood and visits to hospitable friends of the Pachlers occupied much of the time, and Schubert's music was in great demand.

The return journey to Vienna was undertaken on September 24th, and both Jenger and Schubert looked back regretfully on the happy days spent at Gratz. Jenger wrote a letter of thanks to their hostess, and Schubert supplemented it with one to her husband, Dr. Carl Pachler:

"Honoured Sir, I begin to find out already that I was far too happy and comfortable at Gratz, and that Vienna and I don't exactly suit one another. Certainly it is rather big, but on that account empty of all heart, sincerity, candour, genuine thoughts and feelings, rational talk, and utterly lacking in intellectual achievements. One cannot ascertain exactly whether people are clever or stupid, there's such a great deal of petty, poor gossip — real cheerfulness one seldom if ever comes across.

It is very possible, no doubt, that I have myself to blame, being so very slow in the art of thawing. In Gratz I soon learned to appreciate the absence of all artifice and conventional ways; had I stayed longer, I should, of course, have been more profoundly infused with the happiness of such perfect freedom from all restraint.

Coming to particulars, I shall never forget the happy time passed with your dear wife, the sturdy Pachleros and the little Faust.[1] These were the happiest days I have passed for a long time. In the hope of my being able some day to express my gratitude in a fitting manner,

I remain, with the greatest respect,
yours most obediently,
Franz Schubert.

P.S. I hope to send the libretto in a few days."

The libretto mentioned was that of *Alfonso and Estrella*. Schubert had left the score at Gratz in the hope of getting the opera performed there. The Pachlers used their influence in the matter, but without success. The conductor, Hysel, declared that the technical difficulties of the work were insurmountable.

---

[1] Dr. Pachler's only son, aged seven.

The score remained in Dr. Pachler's keeping until 1843, when Ferdinand Schubert sent for it in the hope, which proved fruitless, of obtaining a performance in Vienna.

Madame Pachler begged Schubert to write a piano duet for herself and her little son, and he complied by sending her a march in G, with the following letter:

> "Herewith I forward the four-hand piece for the little Faust. I am afraid it will not meet with your approval, as I do not feel myself particularly well qualified for writing things in this style.
>
> I hope you are both in a better state of health than I am; the pains in my head — a common disorder with me — have returned.
>
> Pray congratulate Dr. Carl heartily for me on his birthday, and let him know that I have not been able as yet to get back from that lazy fellow, Gottdank, my libretto, which I let him have to read through months and months ago.
>
> I remain, with great respect,
> your most obedient,
> Franz Schubert."

This letter is dated October 12th. The pains in his head mentioned by Schubert were symptoms of his approaching illness. He had suffered for years from nervous headache and a rush of blood to the brain, and the attacks were increasing in intensity. No idea of any serious malady, however, seems to have been entertained at this time, either by himself or his friends.

Musically the product of 1827 was at least of equal value to that of previous years. Tho largest choral work was the *Deutsche Messe*, a series of movements set to a text by Johann Philip Neumann, and composed for the Vienna Polytechnic. The accompaniment is for organ, wind instruments, oboes, clarinets, bassoons, horns, trumpets, trombones, and drums.

Acting out a charade, with Schubert at the piano.

In style the music is religious, simple, and homophonous.

The trio in B♭ (D898) was probably, and the trio in E♭ (D929) certainly, composed this year. In the B♭ trio Schubert reverts to a simpler, lighter style of composition than he had lately affected. By some odd caprice of fate, this work enjoys greater popularity than its companion, which is its equal in melodic beauty, and far grander in conception, more poetic, and more thoroughly imbued with Schubert's individuality. The Impromptus for piano (D935), are supposed to have been written about this time; the date of D899 (Opus 90) is unknown.

The completion of the *Winterreise* seems to have occupied his attention in the autumn of this year. These sad but most lovely Lieder are so well known and admired that no discussion of their merits is needed.

The publications extended to D856 (Opus 88), and included the fantasia-sonata in G, and those portions of the operas *Alfonso and Estrella* and *Fierabras* which were deemed worthy to see the light.

Notwithstanding some negotiations, Schubert did not succeed in placing any of his compositions beyond the confines of Vienna. Probst, of Leipsic, wrote early in the year declining the manuscripts forwarded to him, on the grounds that he was concentrating his energies on the issue of a complete edition of the works of Kalkbrenner. It is easy to sneer at the shortsightedness of one who could not foresee the time when Kalkbrenner's name would be all but forgotten, whilst that of Schubert would become a household word. But a publisher, even if he could look into the future, must still deal with the present, and can only go so far in spreading the fame of an author whom the public is slow to recognise.

Perhaps the oddest communication ever received by a composer was that addressed to Schubert by Friedrich Rochlitz, who wished him to set a poem entitled *Der Erste Ton.* After stating that his directions are merely to be taken as hints for general consideration, he proceeds to enter into minute details as follows:

> "Overture, a staccato chord, *fortissimo*, and then perhaps a lengthy sustained passage, for clarinet or horn, with pauses; then, commencing quietly and slowly, illustrated in music more and more gloomy and restless in style, treated harmonically rather than melodically, a kind of chaos, afterwards gradually brightening and developing ... After the words, 'Wiederhall sie nach' the orchestra should have a *tutti*, and so prepare for the great, brilliant, and sublime chorus, 'Drum Preis dir,' which might be lengthened in accordance with the fancy of the composer; the last lines, however, should, as the conclusion of the entire work, be of a peaceful and mild character, avoiding any change in the time or the key."

Rochlitz then further protests against the idea that his suggestions should be taken as in any way binding upon the composer; but he seems to have been unaware that music to have any value at all must be wholly spontaneous. It appears that five years earlier he had requested Beethoven to undertake a setting of the same poem, but had, unsurprisingly, met with a refusal.

Schubert, who was even less amenable to external pressure than Beethoven, likewise declined. Kreissle expresses surprise at this, and suggests that the didactic character of the work, or a fear of plagiarising from Haydn's representation of chaos, may have influenced him.

It is more probable, however, that his independent spirit objected to the notion of writing music to order, for he was not usually particular in his choice of subjects.

7

Great productivity in 1828 — Symphony in C —
Mass in Eb — Schwanengesang — Last sonatas —
Disappointments — His last illness and death.

THE BRIEF AND CHEQUERED LIFE of Franz Schubert was now drawing to its close. We have followed him through momentary gleams of sunshine and weary years of gloom. We have witnessed his friends labouring more earnestly on his behalf than he was capable of doing himself, and we have noted how their noble and unselfish efforts were frequently frustrated, either by public coldness and indifference, or because they were misdirected. And, lastly, we have watched the growth of his genius even to that stage of development which resulted in the production of works, faulty perhaps as regards structural elegance and symmetry, but matchless for poetry and imaginativeness.

Now, just as the power and beauty of Schubert's music were beginning to be felt outside the limited circle of the Viennese *cognoscenti*, fate was about to remove the man whom the world was at that time unable to appreciate at his full value.

Even if Schubert had experienced a premonition of his approaching end, he could not have shown a stronger determination to accomplish as much as possible during the few months yet remaining to him. This extraordinary concentration of energy may have hastened the decay of his

bodily powers; but it proved that the divine fire within him burned more fiercely than ever to the very last, and that only death was capable of quenching it.

In the month of March, he finished his grand Symphony in C, a work which is now the wonder and admiration of the musical world. This glorious piece may not possess the tenderness and lyrical beauty of the unfinished Symphony in B Minor, but it far surpasses that lovely fragment in breadth and grandeur of outline; and, despite its extreme length, musicians who become thoroughly acquainted with it would not sacrifice a single bar.

In another respect it occupies a unique position among Schubert's instrumental works. It has frequently been remarked, with justice, that his final movements are generally weaker than the remainder of the compositions: their length and diffuseness can show a want of discipline, and the constant reiteration of the same ideas produces a sense of weariness even in the most enthusiastic listener.

It is not so in the Ninth Symphony. Here the finale is the crown and glory of the whole work — a movement unequalled for wild surging force and an intensity of energy which in the peroration becomes almost terrific. It is Schubert's apotheosis in music, the most resplendent manifestation of his genius at its zenith.

This great work, as soon as it was completed, was presented to the Gesellschaft der Musikfreunde in return for the testimonial mentioned previously. The parts were copied out, and the symphony placed in rehearsal; but its extreme length, elaboration, and difficulty constituted a fatal barrier to its performance, and Schubert recommended that they should substitute the earlier and simpler Symphony in C, No. 6.

This must have been a great disappointment to him, for he was now fully conscious of his own powers, and declared that Lieder were no longer to occupy his thoughts; from henceforth he would devote himself to opera and symphony. Yet he did not live to hear any of his principal orchestral works performed on an adequate scale.

His modest and retiring disposition had prevented him until now from giving any concerts on his own account; but finally, in response to numerous requests, he gave a private concert at the Musikverein on March 26th.

The programme of this event has not survived, but it consisted entirely of his own compositions and the success was so signal and unqualified that it was at once decided to give another concert at the earliest opportunity.

But it was not to be; the next time a programme of Schubert's music was performed, the composer was cold in his grave. Though he did not live to hear a performance of his last great symphony, he had the gratification of being present at a rendering of his trios by the celebrated Schuppanzigh company of players. The one referred to in the following letter to Anselm Hüttenbrenner, at Gratz, is the trio in Eb.[1]

> "Dearest friend, you will be astonished at my writing to you. So am I; but if I do write, it is on a purely selfish errand. Now, pray listen.
>
> The post of drawing-master at the Normal High School at Gratz is, I perceive, vacant, and candidatures are invited. My brother Carl, whom you may know, would like to obtain the situation. He is a capital landscape painter, and also a good draughtsman.
>
> If you could give me some assistance in this matter I should be eternally grateful to you. My brother is a married man with children: to secure a permanent salaried post would be exceedingly agreeable to him.
>
> I hope things are going favourably with you, and also with your family and your brothers. Remember me very kindly to them all.
>
> Lately a trio of mine for piano, violin, and cello was played at Schuppanzigh's, and was very well received. It was splendidly rendered by Bocklet, Schuppanzigh, and Linke.
>
> Have you written nothing new? By the by, why don't the two songs appear? Bother it! What a nuisance it is!
>
> I reiterate my first request, and please bear in mind that any assistance given to my brother I consider as done to me.
>
> I remain, until death, your devoted friend, Franz Schubert."

---

[1] According to Kreissle. Nottebohm says it was the Bb trio, and that the work in Eb was performed at Schubert's concert by Bocklet, Bohm, and Linke.

The letter to Probst mentioned on p.149.

This letter testifies to his goodness of heart, and also proves conclusively that his mind was not in the clouded condition so apparent four years previously.

The two songs mentioned were *Im Walde* and *Auf der Brücke*, which were to be published in Gratz. The letter is dated January 18th, and the songs appeared in May as Opus 90 (D899). They were the first compositions of Schubert to appear outside Vienna. In the same month the E♭ trio was published by Probst of Leipsic; and these were the only practical proofs of recognition of his ability beyond his native city.

It will be remembered that Probst had written, a few months previously, declining the work sent to him by Schubert. Shortly afterwards, however, he met the composer in Vienna where his worth was beginning to be appreciated, and consequently he reopened negotiations, asking for something in the way of a "song, romance, or vocal concerted piece." But

Schubert cared for none of these things, and offered the trio in E♭, which Probst accepted, without seeing it, at the price of twenty florins sixty kreutzers; though he stated that "a trio is at best an article to keep up the credit of the firm, and we very seldom make any profit out of it."

The trio was duly forwarded, and Probst then wrote again asking for the opus number and the dedication, to which Schubert replied with this strangely abrupt note:

> "Sir, the number of the trio is 100. I most earnestly beg of you that it may be correctly printed: this I am extremely anxious about. The work will be dedicated to those who know how to appreciate it: that is the most advantageous dedication. With all respect, Franz Schubert."

Failing health and irritation caused by continued financial difficulties can alone account for his tone, which is so at variance with his usual pleasant and genial manner.

Schubert had now brought his powers to a climax in the various areas of songs, chamber, orchestral, and sacred composition.

In the latter, his labours were worthily crowned by the Mass in E♭. No reference to this great work is made in the meagre correspondence about this time, and as far as can be ascertained it was not written for any special occasion. Indeed its extreme length is almost fatal to its use in the church service, except on some high and festive occasion of special importance.

It is a curious and probably unexampled thing in music for a composer to be most successful in his first and last efforts in any particular branch of his art. But Schubert's early Mass in F is superior even to the latest of its companions in chaste melody, symmetry of proportion, and a true church-like style; and both the first and last are greater than the intermediate masses in G, C, B♭, and A♭.

Death and the Maiden string quartet, D810.

Notwithstanding his stated wish to devote his talents to the larger forms of composition, he did not relax his energy in songwriting until the very last. The most important work in this area was the collection known as the *Schwanengesang*, consisting of seven songs by Rellstab, six by Heine, and one, *Die Taubenpost*, by Seidl.

The poems by Rellstab were originally sent by the author to Beethoven, who declined them due to illness, but recommended that they should be given to Schubert, which was accordingly done after Beethoven's death. The songs of Heine were composed two or three years earlier, according to Baron von Schönstein, and the statement of the publisher that Nos. 1 to 13 were written in August, 1828, may therefore be partially erroneous. But the 14th of these Lieder, *Die Taubenpost*, was undoubtedly penned in October of this year, and therefore possesses a melancholy distinction as being the last work of the most gifted lyrical composer the world has ever seen.

Schubert's last instrumental compositions were the three piano sonatas in C minor (D958), A (D959), and B♭ (D960), which were written, according to Nottebohm, in September. The sonata in B♭ is dated 26th September, 1828.

Here we cannot but note a slight falling off as compared with the sonatas in A minor (D845 and D784), the fantasia in C, and the fantasia-sonata in G. The most regular and well-proportioned of the last three sonatas is that in A. The first and second movements of the one in C minor are very fine, and there are many beauties in the work in B♭, but the first movement is marred by a diffuseness and dreaminess remarkable even for Schubert. The curious resemblance of the last movement to the corresponding portion of Beethoven's great quartet in B♭ (Opus 130), cannot fail to be noticed.

On the whole, and despite much that is original and beautiful in these sonatas, they suggest the enfeebled condition of their author, whose wondrous imagination was beginning to give way to increasing bodily weakness.

It was Schubert's earnest desire to pay another visit this year to Upper Austria, and afterwards stay for a while with his hospitable friends, the Pachlers, at Gratz.

One feels a sense of indignation at learning that this design was not carried into execution solely because of his impoverished finances. Publication of his smaller pieces went on with tolerable regularity, but the amount of payment was in all instances so pitiably small that he had scarcely sufficient to meet his daily needs. It is well nigh certain that at no period of his life did his annual income amount to £100 of English money at its present valuation.

Although he was forced to abandon his idea of a tour in the mountains of Styria, he still nurtured the hope of visiting Gratz, as we learn from the correspondence which passed between Jenger and the Pachlers; for he seems to have anticipated some more liberal remittances as the result of offers from Schott,

Brüggemann, and other publishers in distant cities.

But this help did not arrive, and on September 25th, he wrote to Jenger:

> "I have already given Haslinger the second portion of the *Winterreise.* It is all over with my excursion to Gratz this year, for my monetary, like the weather prospects, are utterly gloomy and unfavourable. I accept with pleasure the invitation to Dr. Menz, as I should be very glad to hear Baron Schönstein sing. On Saturday afternoon you can meet me at Bogner's Coffee House, Singerstrasse, between four and five o'clock.
>
> Your friend,
> Schubert."

Still another chance presented itself of escaping for a while from the humdrum of Vienna. Franz Lachner, Capellmeister of the Kärnthnerthor Theatre, was asked to supervise the production of his opera, *Die Bürgschaft*, at Pesth. He was friendly with Schubert; and Anton Schindler, Beethoven's biographer, who was resident at Pesth, utilised this circumstance to invite Schubert to be present at the production of the opera. His letter suggests that he was well acquainted with Schubert's character:

> "We propose the following arrangements. You must make up your mind to give a private concert, where your vocal compositions must form the bulk of the programme. People look for a thorough success; and as it is very well known that your shyness and careless habits prevent any large amount of activity and zeal on your part, let me tell you, without hesitation, that every one here will labour cheerfully and enthusiastically to support you,

Beethoven and Schubert were often at Bogner's Coffee House.
In his last two years, Schubert was there practically every evening.

The Green Anchor was a favourite haunt of Schubert's.

Anton Schindler, Beethoven's biographer.

whatever may be the amount of dead weight to be carried.

Still, you must bring a few letters of introduction from and to your aristocratic friends. Lachner thinks there ought to be one from the Esterhazy family, and so do I ... to win safely one hundred florins thus is not a matter to be despised; besides, other advantages may follow in due time.

Well then, up! Be alive! Don't waste time in thinking about it, and don't say no. None of your excuses, mind!

You will be well backed up, and firmly supported ... and so, God be with you!

We all expect that you will be as pliable as possible, and not prove yourself a stubborn animal ..."

Ferdinand Schubert

This was written on October 11th, and Schubert made no reply; doubtless he felt himself already beyond travelling.

Everything seemed now to accelerate the fatal culmination of his increasing weakness. He suffered from attacks of giddiness and headache, and at the recommendation of a physician he left Schober's house, where he had lived for some time, to stay with his brother Ferdinand, who had settled in the Wieden suburb, No. 694 Firmian's Gasse.

Unfortunately the house was new and damp, and instead of getting better, he began at once to get worse. At the beginning of October, however, his condition improved somewhat, and with his brother and two friends, he made a short trip of five days to Unter-Waltersdorf and Eisenstadt.

But shortly after his return to Vienna his appetite entirely deserted him, and from then on he scarcely tasted solid food.

Ferdinand Schubert's home today, where Franz Schubert died.

Still he took walking exercise, and on November 3rd went to hear a performance of a requiem composed by Ferdinand.

Next day he called upon the court organist, Sechter, to arrange with him for some lessons in counterpoint. Herein his native diffidence was once more illustrated, for although it cannot be said that he was a great contrapuntist, yet he knew sufficient of the art to write some effective fugal movements — witness the *Cum sancto Spiritu* in the Mass in F, and the *Et Vitam venturi* in the Mass in E♭.

A week later he was compelled to take to his bed, feeling, as he said, no actual pain, but excessive weakness and depression. About this time he wrote a last letter to Schober:

"Dear Schober, I am ill. I have neither eaten nor drunk anything for eleven days, and shift, weak and weary, from my chair to my bed and back again. If I attempt to eat anything it will not stay in me.

Will you be so kind as to console me in this desperate condition by the loan of some more books? I have read Cooper's *The Last of the Mohicans*, *The Spy*, *The Pilot*, and *The Pioneers*. If you should have any more of his, I implore you to send them to me, or anything else.

Your friend,
Schubert."

Even now he seems to have entertained no serious apprehensions, for he spent a couple of hours in correcting the proof sheets of the *Winterreise*, and even expressed an earnest wish for a new libretto of an opera.

On the 16th there was a consultation of doctors, and it was thought that an attack of typhus fever was at hand. On the evening of the 17th he was quite delirious, but next day he slightly recovered, and asked Ferdinand "What is going to happen to me? What are they doing to me?"

His brother and Dr. Behring spoke words of consolation and hope, but Schubert replied slowly and earnestly,

"No, no, here is my end."

Later he said in an agonised voice,

"I entreat you to carry me to my own room, and don't leave me in this hole in the earth. What! Don't I deserve a place above ground?"

Ferdinand endeavoured to persuade him that he was lying in his own room, but Franz replied,

"No, no, it is not true; Beethoven is not laid here."

Franz Schubert's death mask. Its veracity has been questioned.

This was taken as evidence of his desire to rest near Beethoven, and the wish was reverently respected. At three o'clock on the afternoon of the 19th he passed peacefully away, after an illness which in its serious form had lasted scarcely more than a week.

It cost seventy florins to remove the body to Währing cemetery, and the family could ill afford the expense. Ferdinand said:

> "It is a large sum, a very large sum, but very
> little for the honour of Franz's resting place."

Numbers of his friends came to the house on the 20th and decked his coffin with wreaths and garlands, and a laurel wreath was twisted round his temples.

Next day the funeral took place, Schober being chief mourner. The weather was wet, but a large crowd followed the procession from the parish church, where a musical service was performed, to the Währing Churchyard.

Schubert's current grave in Vienna's Central Cemetery,
to which his remains were relocated in 1880.

Here all that was mortal of Franz Schubert was consigned
to a grave, only separated by three others from that of
Beethoven. Thus the two glorious masters rest side by side in
death, and the world has now agreed to regard the younger
with scarcely less fervent love and admiration than the elder.

The many friends of the deceased master busied themselves
with ardour and unanimity to render every possible honour to
his memory. On November 27th the Kirchenmusik Verein
performed Mozart's *Requiem*, and on December 23rd a requiem
by Anselm Hüttenbrenner was given at the Augustiner Kirche.

There was a general desire to erect a monument over the
grave, and as his father and brothers had exhausted their
means in the expenses of the funeral, a chamber concert was
given at the Musikverein on January 30th for the purpose. This
was so successful that it was repeated, and the net result was

Franz Grillparzer

a profit of 360 florins, a sum sufficient to meet the expense of the Requiem as well as that of the memorial.

The design of the latter was sketched by Schober, and the epitaph was composed by Franz Grillparzer. The sentiment of the opening lines "Here lies buried a rich treasure but yet more glorious hopes," provoked the displeasure of the few who thoroughly comprehended the value of Schubert's work, and their feelings are now shared by musicians universally.

Schubert was indeed developing new powers when death cut him short but the same may be said of Mozart, to a lesser degree of Mendelssohn, and even of Beethoven himself. On the other hand, the labours of Schubert's brief existence have given him a place in music as clear and well defined as that of any of the great masters, and of no less value than the best of them.

Statue of Schubert in Vienna's Stadt Park.

Poster for a 2012 festival of Schubert's music in Heilbronn, Germany.

8

*Posthumous honours — Personal qualities —
Schubert's position in music — General survey of
his works — Recognition of his genius.*

BEFORE WE PROCEED TO CONSIDER the artistic legacy
of Schubert's life, it is necessary to return for a moment
to his personality. We have seen how the coldness and
indifference of the world generally towards him was
compensated for, to some extent, by the hearty sympathy and
love of a few congenial spirits, whose unselfish devotion to his
interests must have given him some consolation for the rebuffs
he had to encounter elsewhere.

The subtle influence which Schubert exercised over those
with whom he was brought into close contact was not to be
accounted for by any graces of person or manner. Kreissle says
that he was under average height, round backed and
shouldered, with plump arms and hands, and short fingers. He
had a round and puffy face, low forehead, thick lips, bushy
eyebrows, and a short turned-up nose. This description does
not coincide with our ideas of one in whom either intellectual
or imaginative qualities are strongly developed.

Add to this the fact that in society Schubert's manner was
awkward, the result of an unconquerable diffidence and
bashfulness when in the presence of strangers. And he was
even less fitted than Beethoven to shine in the salons of the
Viennese aristocracy, for his capacity as an executive musician
was more limited.

But he was far more relaxed among his friends, and perhaps his greatest, and certainly his most frequent pleasure, was to discuss music over a friendly glass in some cosy tavern. It would be entirely unjust to say that he was a drunkard, but he was not over cautious in his potations, and frequently took more than was prudent or consistent with a regard for health. This weakness was purely the result of his fondness for genial society, for he was not a solitary drinker, and invariably devoted the early portion of the day to work.

The enormous mass of his compositions sufficiently proves his capacity for hard and unremitting labour, and no diminution of energy was observable to the very last.

It is not easy for us at this distance of time, and with our colder northern temperament, to comprehend the romantic feelings of attachment that existed between Schubert and some of his friends — feelings which, however, are by no means rare among the impulsive youth of South Germany — but his naive simplicity, cheerful and eminently sociable disposition, insensibility to envy, and incorruptible modesty, were qualities quite able to transform the respect due to his genius into a strong personal liking.

Schubert was in truth a child of nature, one whom to know was to love; for his faults might be summed up into a general incapacity to understand his own interests, and it might be said of him as truly as of anyone that he was no man's enemy save his own; thus reversing Shakespeare's words — the good which he did lives after him; the evil was interred with his bones.

The services Schubert rendered to art may best be estimated by imagining for an instant the gap which would be created were his work to be blotted out of existence. In the cursory observations on his compositions in these pages, less prominence has been given to his Lieder than to his works in other forms of music. This has been done deliberately, for although, happily, it is no longer the custom to consider

Schubert exclusively or principally as a songwriter, yet the extent and value of his larger works are still imperfectly recognised, and much splendid music has still to see light.

But when all has been said, it is as the monarch of the Lieder that Schubert's greatness and individuality shine forth most distinctly. But his is not the place to enter upon a lengthy discussion of the characteristics of the German Lieder, as interesting as such an inquiry might be.

In its history of national, or more properly speaking, folk music, Germany is richer than any other nation; but various causes had combined to produce a period of depression, and in southern Germany the influence of Italian opera had for a while crushed the Lied as a form of art.

The genius of Haydn, Mozart, and Beethoven struggled not altogether effectually against this anti-national feeling, but a reaction had already commenced, and Schubert flourished precisely at the right moment to take advantage of the treasures of modern German poetry created by Goethe, Heine, and others in whom the true Teutonic fire burst forth.

It has been said, by one who wrote enthusiastically of Schubert, that he would gradually have set the whole of German literature to music had he lived long enough. He had but to read a poem once or twice, and its most appropriate expression by means of music came to him readily, and without further mental effort.

It was of course impossible for him to evoke beautiful ideas from worthless verse, and among his 600 songs we find side by side with some of supreme loveliness others of scarcely any value. This arises from the fact that he was perfectly indifferent as to his materials, his fertile imagination constantly hungering to link itself with some shape or form, whether beautiful or commonplace. It is in the *durchcomponirtes* or 'through-composed' Lied, as opposed to the strophic Lied, that his genius was most fully displayed.

Our English ballad is a tolerably close equivalent of the latter, but in the former each line of the poem suggests its own musical illustration, though without any intrusion of recitative or sacrifice of rhythm.

An extensive volume could be written about Schubert's Lieder, and the best evidence of their power lies in the influence they have had on later composers who have worked in the same direction. Mendelssohn's songs, despite their melodic and purely lyrical beauty, are somewhat lacking in depth, but Schumann understood thoroughly the poetic significance of the Lied.

Among living musicians Robert Franz — a composer too little recognised in this country — has laboured most effectively in this domain.

If in other branches of composition Schubert did not succeed in founding a school, he nevertheless made his mark, which thoughtful musicians cannot fail to recognise. His use of the orchestra is tinged with a decided individuality, more especially in his treatment of the wind instruments. The delicious writing for the wood in the *andante con moto* of the Unfinished Symphony will recur to the minds of musicians, and the colouring produced by *piano* harmonies of the brass in some of his works is altogether novel. This feeling for the tender and melancholy in orchestration must have been intuitive, as he had no opportunity of testing his effects in his later and nobler works.

The beauty and poetry of the last quartets, trios, and piano sonatas have never been equalled, much less surpassed, and the 'heavenly length,' want of proportion and diffuseness of some of the movements, cease, after due familiarity, to detract from the charm, particularly as certain of the more prominent composers of the present day are prone to indulge in these faults to even greater excess.

It has already been pointed out that Schubert comparatively failed in operatic composition, partly as a consequence of his own peculiar idiosyncrasies, and partly because he was singularly unfortunate in the subjects given him to set. We cannot advise the revival of his lyric dramas on the stage, but the scores of these works should be published, especially *Alfonso and Estrella* and *Fierabras*, as they doubtless contain many gems which would prove most attractive in the concert room.

In the realm of church music, Schubert was far more successful. The Masses in F, G, and Eb are superior in refinement and true religious style to any of Haydn or Mozart, the Requiem of the latter excepted; and they may worthily take rank with Beethoven's setting of the sacred office in C. Schubert's Mass in F, composed at the age of seventeen, is as remarkable an evidence of early genius as any of the better known works of Mendelssohn's boyhood.

It may be said of Schubert, more truly than of any other composer, that his history, in one sense, began only after he died. His comparatively sudden and unexpected death caused an outburst of grief among those who knew him best, and the various means taken to express this feeling have been here recorded. But these demonstrations were no more than are frequently paid to musicians who have acquired some local fame, and whom admirers and friends would fain persuade the world to accept as men of genius.

A large number of compositions were placed by his relatives with Diabelli, and publication proceeded steadily for some five or six years; but after 1830 the stream consisted chiefly of songs and other vocal works, after which it almost dried up.

The Lieder penetrated to France, where they became popular, and from there a few examples made their way to England. There seemed now a probability that Schubert's fame would rest entirely upon his songs, but the mantle of genius had meanwhile descended upon two musicians who were led by instinct to inquire more particularly into a noble heritage that had been left uncared for.

In 1838 Schumann visited Vienna, and took the opportunity to examine the stores of music in the possession of Ferdinand Schubert. Among these was the score of the great Symphony in C, which Schuman persuaded Ferdinand to send to Leipsic.

Mendelssohn, who was conductor of the Gewandhaus concerts at the time, was enchanted with the work, and it was performed for the first time on March 22nd, 1839. The Leipsic public, far more intelligent than that of Vienna, at once recognised its worth, and it soon became a stock favourite. Yet in spite of this the symphony was not heard in Vienna until 1850, when it met with a cold reception. Truly, a prophet has no honour in his own country.

In 1844 Mendelssohn brought the work to London, in the hope of introducing it at the Philharmonic concerts. But at the rehearsal the members of the orchestra made such wry faces, and the few listeners expressed such unfavourable opinions, that he withdrew it angrily, together with his own overture to *Ruy Blas.*

Thanks to the advocacy of Schumann and Mendelssohn his works gradually became known on the Continent, but his proper position in England dates from the establishment of the Monday Popular and Crystal Palace concerts.

Owing in the first instance to the unceasing efforts of Mr. George Grove, it may be said that nowhere did the music of Schubert meet with more appreciation than by the English public, when it had once been properly placed before them. It was even said a few years later that there was now greater danger of Schubert being over rather than underestimated.

That could scarcely be the case.

Clarity of outline, conciseness, and formal beauty are excellent things in musical works, but an exquisite fancy, a noble imagination, and a lofty poetic spirit are of infinitely greater account; and no one ever possessed these inestimable gifts in richer profusion than Franz Schubert.

THE WORKS

The following list is ordered according to 'D numbers'. The list originally published in the 1892 edition of this book is now considerably out of date, and has been replaced by the following more complete catalogue. It is based on the compilation of Schubert's works by the Austrian musicologist Otto Erich Deutsch. It is from this catalogue that the D numbers universally used to identify Schubert's pieces are drawn.

D1   Fantasia in G for Piano Duet.

D2   String Quartet in G (fragment).

D2a   Overture in D for orchestra; was D996.

D2b   Fragment of a Symphony in D; was D997.

D2c   Fragment of a String Quartet in D/F; was D998.

D2d   Six minuets for piano; was D995.

D2e   Fantasia in C for piano; was D993.

D2f   Trio of a minuet in C (sketch).

D3   Movements for String Quartet (published in 1978).

D4   Overture to *Der Teufel als Hydraulicus*.

D5   Song: *Hagar's Klage*.

D6   Song: *Des Mädchens Klage*.

D7   Song: *Eine Leichenphantasie*.

D8   Overture for String Quintet in C (published in 1970).

D8a   Overture for String Quartet in D (arrangement of D8).

D9   Fantasia in G for Piano duet.

D10   Song: *Der Vatermörder.*

D11   Operetta *Der Spiegelritter* (first act only; incomplete).

D12   Overture in D for Orchestra.

D13   Fugue in D (not printed).

D14   Overture for Piano (lost).

D15   Song: *Der Geistertanz* (two fragmentary sketches).

D16   Exercises in imitation.

D17   Settings of *Quel' innocente figlio* for various voices (exercises for Salieri).

D18   String Quartet, No. 1 (in mixed keys).

D19   String Quartet (in mixed keys) (lost).

D19a   String Quartet (in mixed keys) (lost).

D19b   Waltzes and March (lost).

D20   Overture for String Quartet in B♭ (lost).

D21   Six Variations in E♭ (lost).

D22   Twelve Minuets with Trios (lost).

D23   Song: *Klaglied.*

D24   Variations in F (unpublished).

D24a   Fugue in C (for organ?).

D24b   Fugue in G (for organ?).

D24c   Fugue in D (for organ?).

D24d   Fugue in C for piano (fragment).

D24e   Mass (in F?) (fragment).

D25   Exercises in Counterpoint (not printed).

D25c   Fugue in F for piano (fragment).

D26	Overture in D for Orchestra.
D27	Salve Regina in F for Soprano, Orchestra, and Organ.
D28	Trio in B♭, called Sonata for Piano, Violin, and Cello.
D29	Andante in C for Piano (arrangement of String Quartet, No. 3).
D30	Song: *Der Jüngling am Bache.*
D31	Kyrie to a Mass in D for Chorus, Orchestra and Organ.
D32	String Quartet, No. 2 in C.
D33	Settings of *Entra l'uomo allor che nasce* for various voices.
D34	Setting of *Te solo adoro* for four mixed voices (exercise for Salieri).
D35	Setting of *Serbate, o Dei custodi* for various voices (exercise for Salieri).
D36	String Quartet, No. 3 in B♭.
D37	Song: *Die Advokaten.*
D37a	Fugal sketches in B♭; was D967.
D38	Trio: *Totengräberlied.*
D39	Sketch of a song: *Ich sass an einer Tempelhalle am Musenhain* (not printed).
D39a	Three minuets and trios (lost).
D40	String Quartet in E♭ (lost), possibly identical with D87.
D41	Minuets with Trios for Piano (in an 'easy style').
D41a	Fugue in E for piano (fragment).
D42	Song: *Misero pargoletto.*

D43 Trio: *Dreifach ist der Schritt der Zeit.*

D44 Song: *Totengräberlied.*

D45 Kyrie in B♭.

D46 String Quartet, No. 4 in C.

D47 Song for mixed chorus with tenor soli and piano: *Dithyrambe* (fragment).

D48 Fantasia in C for Piano Duet (called *Grande Sonate*).

D49 Kyrie in D for Chorus and Orchestra (fragment).

D50 Song: *Die Schatten.*

D51 Trio: *Unendliche Freude.*

D52 Song: *Sehnsucht* (first version, second version is D636).

D53 Trio: *Vorüber die stöhnende Klage.*

D54 Canon: *Unendliche Freude.*

D55 Trio: *Selig durch die Liebe.*

D56 Sanctus: Canon for three voices in B♭.

D57 Trio: *Hier strecket der wallende Pilger.*

D58 Trio: *Dessen Fahne Donnerstürme wallte.*

D59 Song: *Verklärung.*

D60 Trio: *Hier umarmen sich getreue Gatten.*

D61 Song: *Ein jugendlicher Maienschwung.*

D62 Trio: *Thronend auf erhabnem Sitz.*

D63 Trio: *Wer die steile Sternenbahn.*

D64 Trio: *Majestät'sche Sonnenrosse.*

D65 Canon: *Schmerz verzerret ihr Gesicht.*

D66 Kyrie in F for Chorus, Orchestra, and Organ.

D67   Trio: *Frisch atmet des Morgens lebendiger Hauch.*

D68   String Quartet, No. 5 in B♭ (two Allegro movements, others probably lost).

D69   Canon: *Dreifach ist der Schritt der Zeit*, for three voices.

D70   Canon: *Ewig still steht die Vergangenheit,* for three voices.

D71   Trio: *Die zwei Tugendwege.*

D71a   Canon: *Alleluja* in F.

D71b   Fugue in E for piano (fragment).

D71c   Fragment of an Orchestral Score in D; was D966a.

D72   Minuet and finale in F of an Octet for Winds.

D72a   Allegro in F for wind octet (unfinished).

D73   Song: *Thekla.*

D74   String Quartet, No. 6 in D.

D75   Drinking song, for bass solo with male chorus and piano.

D76   Song: *Pensa, che questo istante.*

D77   Song: *Der Taucher* (first version, second is D111).

D78   Song: *Son fra l'onde.*

D79   *Eine kleine Trauermusik* for wind instruments.

D80   *Kantate zur Namensfeier des Vaters* for three male voices and guitar.

D81   Song: *Auf den Sieg der Deutschen* (accompaniment of two violins and cello).

D82   Symphony No. 1 in D major.

D83   Song: *Zur Namensfeier des Herrn Andreas Siller* with violin and harp.

D84   Opera: *Des Teufels Lustschloß* (23 numbers).

D85   Offertory in C (fragment), not printed.

D86   Minuet in D for String Quartet.

D87   String Quartet, No. 10 in E♭.

D87a   Andante in C (for string quartet?).

D88   Canon: *Verschwunden sind die Schmerzen.*

D89   Five Minuets with six Trios for String Quartet.

D90   Five *Deutsche Tänze* with Coda and seven Trios
       for String Quartet.

D91   Two Minuets and Four Trios for Piano (unpublished).

D92   Canon for Two Voices (lost).

D93   Three songs of Don Gayseros.

D94   String Quartet, No. 7 in D.

D94a   Orchestral fragment in B♭.

D94b   Five minuets and six Deutsche with trios (lost).

D95   Song: *Adelaide.*

D96   Quartet in G for flute, guitar, viola and cello
       (arrangement of Wenzel Thomas Matiegka's *Notturno*
       for flute, viola and guitar, Op. 21).

D97   Song: *Trost. An Elisa.*

D98   Song: *Erinnerung.*

D99   Song: *Andenken.*

D100   Song: *Geisternähe.*

D101   Song: *Erinnerung (Totenopfer).*

D102   Song: *Die Betende.*

D103   String Quartet in C.

D104   Song: *Die Befreier Europa's in Paris.*

D105   Mass, No. 1 in F.

D106   Salve Regina in B♭ for Tenor, Orchestra, and Organ.

D107   Song: *Lied aus der Ferne.*

D108   Song: *Der Abend.*

D109   Song: *Lied der Liebe.*

D110   Cantata: *Wer ist gross?*
         For bass solo and chorus with orchestra.

D111   Song: *Der Taucher* (second version, first is D77).

D111a String trio in B♭ (fragment), lost.

D112   String Quartet, No. 8 in B♭.

D113   Song: *An Emma.*

D114   Song: *Romanze.*

D115   Song: *An Laura, als sie Klopstocks Auferstehunglied sang.*

D116   Song: *Der Geistertanz.*

D117   Song: *Das Mädchen aus der Fremde.*

D118   Song: *Gretchen am Spinnrade*, Op. 2.

D119   Song: *Nachtgesang.*

D120   Song: *Trost in Tränen.*

D121   Song: *Schäfers Klagelied*, Op. 3, No. 1 (two versions).

D122   Song: *Ammenlied.*

D123   Song: *Sehnsucht* (two versions).

D124   Song: *Am See.*

D125   Symphony in B♭.

D126 Song: *Szene aus Goethe's Faust.*

D127 Canon: *Selig alle, die im Herrn entschlafen* (lost).

D128 Twelve *Wiener Deutsche Tänze* for Piano.

D129 Trio: *Mailied.*

D130 Canon for three voices: *Der Schnee zerrinnt.*

D131 Two Canons for three voices: *Lacrimoso son io.*

D132 Trio: *Lied beim Rundtanz* (lost).

D133 Trio: *Lied im Freien* (lost).

D134 Song: *Ballade.*

D135 Trio in A for Piano to a Waltz. See D139.

D136 *Erstes Offertorium* in C for Soprano, Tenor, Clarinet or Violin Concertante, Orchestra, and Organ.

D137 Opera: *Adrast* (fragment), thirteen numbers only.

D138 Song: *Rastlose Liebe*, Op. 5, No. 1.

D139 Walzer in C# for Piano with Trio in A.

D141 Song: *Klage um Ali Bey.*

D142 Song: *Der Mondabend.*

D142 Song: *Geistes-Gruß.*

D143 Song: *Genügsamkeit.*

D144 Song: *Romanze.*

D145 Twelve Walzer, seventeen Ländler, and nine Écossaises for piano, Opus18.

D146 Twenty Walzer for Piano, called *Letzte Walzer.*

D147 Trio: *Bardengesang.*

D148 Song: *Trinklied.*

D149 Song: *Der Sänger (Was hör ich draußen vor der Tür)*.

D150 Song: *Loda's Gespenst*.

D151 Song: *Auf einen Kirchhof*.

D152 Song: *Minona*.

D153 Song: *Als ich sie erröten sah*.

D154 Allegro in E for Piano. First movement of a sonata.

D155 Song: *Das Bild*.

D156 Ten Variations in F for Piano.

D157 Sonata (No. 1) in E for Piano.

D158 Écossaise in F for Piano.

D159 Song: *Die Erwartung*.

D160 Song: *Am Flusse*.

D161 Song: *An Mignon*, Op. 19, No. 2.

D162 Song: *Nähe des Geliebten*, Op. 5, No. 2.

D163 Song: *Sängers Morgenlied*.

D164 Song: *Liebesrausch*, first version, fragment, second version is D179.

D165 Song: *Sängers Morgenlied*.

D166 Song: *Amphiaraos*.

D167 Mass No. 2 in G (the *Mass in G*).

D168 Quartet: *Begräbnislied*.

D168a Osterlied. Formerly D987.

D169 Unison song: *Trinklied vor der Schlacht*.

D170 Song with chorus: *Schwertlied*.

D171 Song: *Gebet während der Schlacht*.

D172   Song: *Der Morgenstern.*

D173   String Quartet, No. 9 in G.

D174   Song: *Das war ich.*

D175   Stabat Mater in G for chorus, orchestra, and organ.

D176   Song: *Die Sterne.*

D177   Song: *Vergebliche Liebe.*

D178   Adagio in G for Piano (two versions).

D179   Song: *Liebesrausch.* Second version.

D180   Song: *Sehnsucht der Liebe.*

D181   Offertory in A for chorus, orchestra, and organ.

D182   Song: *Die erste Liebe.*

D183   Song: *Trinklied.*

D184   Gradual in C for chorus, orchestra, and organ.

D185   Second Dona, No. is for the Mass in F, for Quartet with mixed chorus, orchestra, and organ for D105.

D186   Song: *Die Sterbende.*

D187   Song: *Stimme der Liebe.*

D188   Song: *Naturgenuss.*

D189   Song: *An die Freude.*

D190   Singspiel: *Der vierjährige Posten, No. 5 Gott! höre meine Stimme.*

D191   Song: *Der Mädchens Klage.*

D192   Song: *Der Jüngling am Bache.*

D193   Song: *An den Mond.*

D194   Song: *Die Mainacht.*

D195   Song: *Amalia.*

D196   Song: *An die Nachtigall.*

D197   Song: *An die Apfelbäume, wo ich Julien erblickte.*

D198   Song: *Seufzer.*

D199   *Mailied:* for two voices or two horns.

D200   Symphony No. 3 in D major.

D201   Song: *Auf den Tod einer Nachtigall.*

D202   Mailied: for two voices or two horns.

D203   *Der Morgenstern* for two voices or two horns.

D204   *Jägerlied* for two voices or two horns.

D205   *Lützow's wilde Jagd* for two voices or two horns.

D206   Song: *Liebeständelei.*

D207   Song: *Der Liebende.*

D208   Song: *Die Nonne.* First version.

D209   Song: *Der Liedler.*

D210   Song: *Die Liebe (Freudvoll und Liedvoll).*

D211   Song: *Adelwold und Emma.*

D212   Song: *Die Nonne.* Second version.

D213   Song: *Der Traum.*

D214   Song: *Die Laube.*

D215   Song: *Jägers Abendlied.* First version, second is D368.

D216   Song: *Meeres Stille*, Op. 3, No. 2.

D217   Song: *Colma's Klage.*

D218   Song: *Grablied.*

D219   Song: *Das Finden.*

D220 Singspiel: *Fernando.* In one act, 7 numbers.

D221 Song: *Der Abend.*

D222 Song: *Lieb Minna.*

D223 Salve Regina (Zweites Offertorium) in F for soprano, orchestra, and organ (two versions).

D224 Song: *Wandrers Nachtlied* Op. 4, No. 3.

D225 Song: *Der Fischer*, Op. 5, No. 3.

D226 Song: *Erster Verlust*, Op. 5, No. 4.

D227 Song: *Idens Nachtgesang.*

D228 Song: *Von Ida.*

D229 Song: *Die Erscheinung.*

D230 Song: *Die Täuschung.*

D231 Song: *Das Sehnen.*

D232 Quartet: *Hymne an den Unendlichen.*

D233 Song: *Geist der Liebe.*

D234 Song: *Tischlied.*

D235 Song: *Abends unter der Linde.*

D236 Song: *Das Abendrot* for three voices with piano.

D237 Song: *Abends unter der Linde.*

D238 Song: *Die Mondnacht.*

D239 Singspiel: *Claudine von Villa Bella* (incomplete).

1. *Das hast du wohl bereitet.*

2. *Fröhlicher, seliger, herrlicher Tag!*

3. *Hin und wieder fliegen die Pfeile.*

4. *Alle Freuden alle Gaben.*

5. *Es erhebt sich eine Stimme.*

6. *Liebe schwärmt auf allen Wegen.*

7. *Mit Mädchen sich vertragen.*

8. *Deinem Willen nachzugeben.*

9. *Liebliches Kind, kannst du mir sagen.*

10. *Mich umfängt ein banger Schauer.*

D240 Song: *Huldigung.*

D241 Song: *Alles um Liebe.*

D242a Song: *Winterlied* (fragment).

D245 Song: *An den Frühling.*

D246 Song: *Die Bürgschaft.*

D247 Song: *Die Spinnerin.*

D248 Song: *Lob des Tokayers.*

D249 Cantata: *Die Schlacht* (sketch), not printed. Second sketch is D387.

D250 Song: *Das Geheimnis.*

D251 Song: *Hoffnung* First version, second is D637.

D252 Song: *Das Mädchen aus der Fremde.* Second setting, first setting is D117.

D253   Song: *Punschlied. Im Norden zu singen.*

D254   Song: *Der Gott und die Bajadere.*

D255   Song: *Der Rattenfänger.*

D256   Song: *Der Schatzgräber.*

D257   Song: *Heidenröslein,* Op. 3, No. 3.

D258   Song: *Bundeslied.*

D259   Song: *An den Mond.*

D260   Song: *Wonne der Wehmut.*

D261   Song: *Wer kauft Liebesgötter?*

D262   Song: *Die Fröhlichkeit.*

D263   Song: *Cora an die Sonne.*

D264   Song: *Der Morgenkuss.*

D265   Song: *Abendständchen. An Lina.*

D266   Song: *Morgenlied.*

D267   Quartet: *Trinklied.*

D268   Quartet: *Bergknappenlied.*

D269   Trio: *Das Leben.*

D270   Song: *An die Sonne.*

D271   Song: *Der Weiberfreund.*

D272   Song: *An die Sonne.*

D273   Song: *Lilla an die Morgenröte.*

D274   Song: *Tischlerlied.*

D275   Song: *Totenkranz für ein Kind.*

D276   Song: *Abendlied.*

D277   Trio: *Punschlied.*

D278   Song: *Ossians Lied nach dem Falle Nathos.*

D279   Sonata No. 2 in C.

D280   Song: *Das Rosenband.*

D281   Song: *Das Mädchen von Inistore.*

D282   Song: *Cronnan.*

D283   Song: *An den Frühling.*

D284   Song: *Lied.*

D285   Song: *Furcht der Geliebten.*

D286   Song: *Selma und Selmar.*

D287   Song: *Vaterlandslied.*

D288   Song: *An Sie.*

D289   Song: *Die Sommernacht.*

D290   Song: *Die frühen Gräber.*

D291   Song: *Dem Unendlichen.*

D291b Song: *Dem Unendlichen.*

D292   Song: *Klage.*

D293   Song: *Shilric und Vinvela.*

D294   *Namensfeier für Franz Michael Vierhalter.*

D295   Song: *Hoffnung.*

D296   Song: *An den Mond.*

D297   Song: *Augenlied.*

D298   Song: *Liane.*

D299   Twelve Écossaises for Piano.

D300   Song: *Der Jüngling an der Quelle.*

D301   Song: *Lambertine.*

D302   Song: *Labetrank der Liebe.*

D303   Song: *An die Geliebte.*

D304   Song: *Wiegenlied.*

D305   Song: *Mein Gruss an den Mai.*

D306   Song: *Skolie.*

D307   Song: *Die Sternenwelten.*

D308   Song: *Die Macht der Liebe.*

D309   Song: *Das gestörte Glück.*

D310   Song: *Sehnsucht* (two versions).

D311   Song: *An den Mond.*

D312   Song: *Hektors Abschied.*

D313   Song: *Die Sterne.*

D314   Song: *Nachtgesang.*

D315   Song: *An Rosa I.*

D316   Song: *An Rosa II.*

D317   Song: *Idens Schwanenlied.*

D318   Song: *Schwanengesang.*

D319   Song: *Luisens Antwort.*

D320   Song: *Der Zufriedene.*

D321   Song: *Kennst du das Land?*

D321   Song: *Mignon.*

D322   Song: *Hermann und Thusnelda.*

D323   Song: *Klage der Ceres.*

D324   Mass, No. 3 in B♭.

D325   Song: *Harfenspieler I.*

D326   Singspiel: *Die Freunde von Salamanka.* 18 numbers.

D327   Song: *Lorma.*

D328   Song: *Erlkönig.* Opus 1, 1815.

D329   Song: *Die drei Sänger.*

D329a   Sketch of a quartet: *Das Grab.*

D330   Song: *Das Grab.* First version.
        Second is D377, third is D569.

D331   Quartet: *Der Entfernten.*

D332   Quartet: *Der Entfernten* (lost).

D333   Trio: *Lass dein Vertrauen nicht schwinden* (lost).

D334   Minuet in A with Trio for Piano.

D335   Minuet in E with two Trios for Piano.

D336   Minuet in D with Trio for Piano.

D337   Song for male chorus: *Die Einsiedelei.*

D338   Song for male chorus: *An den Frühling.*

D339   Trio: *Amor's Macht* (lost).

D340   Trio: *Badelied* (lost).

D341   Trio: *Sylphen* (lost).

D342   Song: *Seraphine an ihr Klavier* called *An mein Klavier.*

D343   Song: *Am Tage Aller Seelen*
        called *Litanei auf das Fest Aller Seelen.*

D344 Song: *Am ersten Maimorgen* (unpublished).

D345 Konzertstück (concert piece), in D for Violin, String Quartet, two Oboes, two Trumpets & Timpani.

D346 Allegretto in C for Piano (fragment).

D347 Allegro moderato in C for Piano (fragment).

D348 Andantino in C for Piano (fragment).

D349 Adagio in C for Piano (fragment).

D350 Song: *Der Entfernten*.

D351 Song: *Fischerlied*.

D352 Song: *Licht und Liebe* called *Nachtgesang*.

D353 String Quartet, No. 11 in E.

D354 Four *Kornische Ländler* in D.

D355 Eight Ländler in F# for Piano.

D356 Quartet: *Trinklied*.

D357 Canon: *Gold'ner Schein* for three voices.

D358 Song: *Die Nacht*.

D359 Song: *Lied der Mignon*.

D360 Song: *Lied eines Schiffers an die Dioskuren*.

D361 Song: *Am Bach im Frühlinge*.

D362 Song: *Lied*. First version, second is D501.

D363 Song: *An Chloen* (fragment), not printed.

D364 Quartet: *Fischerlied*.

D365 36 Originaltänze for Piano, Op. 9.

D366 Seventeen *Deutsche Tänze*, called *Ländler*, for Piano.

D367   Song: *Der König in Thule*, Op. 5, No. 5.

D368   Song: *Jägers Abendlied*. Second version, Op. 3, No. 4.

D369   Song: *An Schwager Kronos*, Op. 19, No. 1.

D370   Eight Ländler in D for Piano.

D371   Song: *Klage*.

D372   Song: *An die Natur*.

D373   Song: *Lied*.

D374   Six Ländler in B♭ for violin solo.

D375   Song: *Der Tod Oskar's*.

D376   Song: *Lorma*.

D377   Song: *Das Grab*, called *Das stille Land*.

D378   Eight Ländler in B♭ for Piano.

D379   Deutsches Salve Regina, in F.

D380   Two Minuets with a Trio to each, for piano.

D381   Song: *Morgenlied*.

D382   Song: *Abendlied*.

D383   Stabat Mater in F.

D384   Sonatina in D for Piano and Violin, Op. posth. 137, No. 1.

D385   Sonatina in a for Piano and Violin, Op. posth. 137, No. 2.

D386   Salve Regina in B♭.

D387   Cantata: *Die Schlacht* (sketch).

D388   Song: *Laura am Klavier* (two versions).

D389   Song: *Des Mädchens Klage*. Third version.
        First is D6, second is D191.

D390   Song: *Entzückung an Laura.*
        First version. Second is D577.

D391   Song: *Die vier Weltalter.*

D392   Song: *Pflügerlied.*

D393   Song: *Die Einsiedelei.*

D394   Song: *Gesang an die Harmonie* called *An die Harmonie.*

D395   Song: *Lebensmelodien.*

D396   Song: *Gruppe aus dem Tartarus.*
        First version, fragment, not printed.

D397   Song: *Ritter Toggenburg.*

D398   Song: *Frühlingslied.*

D399   Song: *Auf den Tod einer Nachtigall.*

D400   Song: *Die Knabenzeit.*

D401   Song: *Winterlied.*

D402   Song: *Der Flüchtling.*

D403   Song: *Lied (Ins stille Land)* (two versions).

D404   Song: *Wehmut* called *Die Herbstnacht.*

D405   Song: *Der Herbstabend.*

D406   Song: *Abschied von der Harfe.*

D407   Cantata: *Beitrag zur fünfzigjährigen Jubelfeier des Herrn Salieri.* First version, second is D441.

D408   Sonatina in G for Piano and Violin, Op. posth. 137, No. 3.

D409   Song: *Die verfehlte Stunde* (two versions).

D410   Song: *Sprache der Liebe.*

D411   Song: *Daphne am Bach.*

D412 Song: *Stimme der Liebe*.

D413 Song: *Entzückung*.

D414 Song: *Geist der Liebe*.

D415 Song: *Klage*.

D416 Song: *Lied in der Abwesenheit*.

D417 Symphony No. 4 in C minor (*Tragic*).

D418 Song: *Stimme der Liebe*.

D419 Song: *Julius an Theone*.

D420 Twelve Deutsche Tänze for Piano.

D421 Six Écossaises for Piano.

D422 Quartet: *Naturgenuss*, Op. 16, No. 2.

D423 Trio: *Andenken*.

D424 Trio: *Erinnerung*.

D425 Trio: *Lebenslied* (lost).

D426 Trio *Trinklied* (lost).

D427 Trio: *Trinklied im Mai*.

D428 Trio: *Widerhall*.

D429 Song: *Minnelied*.

D430 Song: *Die frühe Liebe*.

D431 Song: *Blumenlied*.

D432 Song: *Der Leidende* called *Klage* (two versions).

D433 Song: *Seligkeit* called *Minnelied*.

D434 Song: *Erntelied*.

D435 Opera: *Die Bürgschaft*.
      In three acts, unfinished, 16 numbers.

D436   Song: *Klage*. First version, second is D437.

D437   Song: *Klage*. Second version, unpublished.

D438   Rondo in A for Violin and String Quartet.

D439   Quartet: *An die Sonne*.

D440   *Chor der Engel* for mixed chorus.

D441   Trio: *Beitrag zur fünfzigjährigen Jubelfeier des Herrn Salieri* for two tenors and bass with piano. Second version, first is D407.

D442   Song: *Das große Halleluja*.

D443   Song: *Schlachtgesang* called *Schlachtlied*.

D444   Song: *Die Gestirne*.

D445   Song: *Edone*.

D446   Song: *Die Liebesgötter*.

D447   Song: *An den Schlaf*.

D448   Song: *Gott im Frühling*.

D449   Song: *Der gute Hirt*.

D450   Song: *Fragment aus dem Aeschylus* (two versions).

D451   Cantata: *Prometheus* for the nameday of Heinrich Josef Watteroth.

D452   Mass No. 4 in C. Second Benedictus is D961.

D453   Requiem in C minor (fragment) of 64 bars, not published.

D454   Song: *Grablied auf einen Soldaten*.

D455   Song: *Freude der Kinderjahre*.

D456   Song: *Das Heimweh*.

D457   Song: *An die untergehende Sonne*.

D458   Song: *Aus Diego Manazares.*

D459   Sonata, No. 3 in E, called *Fünf Klavierstücke.*

D460   Tantum ergo in C for chorus, orchestra, and organ.

D461   Tantum ergo in C for soli, chorus, and orchestra.

D462   Song: *An Chloen.*

D463   Song: *Hochzeit-Lied.*

D463   Song: *Hochzeitslied.*

D464   Song: *In der Mitternacht.*

D465   Song: *Trauer der Liebe.*

D466   Song: *Die Perle.*

D467   Song: *Pflicht und Liebe.*

D468   Song: *An den Mond.*

D469   Song: *Mignon* (two versions, incomplete).

D470   Overture in B♭ for orchestra.

D471   Trio for Strings in B♭.

D472   *Kantate zu Ehren von Josef Spendou*
        for solo voices, chorus and orchestra.

D473   Song: *Liedesend.*

D474   Song: *Lied des Orpheus, als er in die Hölle ging*
        called *Orpheus.*

D475   Song: *Abschied (nach einer Wallfahrtsarie).*

D476   Song: *Rückweg.*

D477   Song: *Alte Liebe rostet nie.*

D478   Song: *Harfenspieler I,* Op. 12, No. 1 (two versions).

D479   Song: *Harfenspieler II,* Op. 12, No. 3 (two versions).

D480   Song: *Harfenspieler III*, Op. 12, No. 2 (three versions).

D481   Song: *Lied der Mignon*. Fourth version.
       Others are D310, D359, D877.

D482   Song: *Der Sänger am Felsen*.

D483   Song: *Lied (Ferne von der großen Stadt)*.

D484   Song: *Gesang der Geister über den Wassern* (fragment).

D485   Symphony No. 5 in B♭ major.

D486   Magnificat in C.

D487   Adagio & Rondo Concertante in F
       for piano, violin, viola, and cello.

D488   Duet: *Auguste jam coelestium*
       for soprano and tenor with orchestra.

D489   Song: *Der Unglückliche* called *Der Wanderer*.
       First version.

D490   Song: *Der Hirt*.

D491   Song: *Geheimnis*.

D492   Song: *Zum Punsche*.

D493   Song: *Der Wanderer*. Second version, Op. 4, No. 1.

D494   *Der Geistertanz* for chorus.

D495   Song: *Abendlied der Fürstin*.

D496   Song: *Bei dem Grabe meines Vaters*.

D497   Song: *An die Nachtigall*.

D498   Song: *Wiegenlied. Schlafe, schlafe, holder, süßer Knabe*.

D499   Song: *Abendlied*.

D500   Song: *Phidile*.

D501　Song: *Zufriedenheit.*

D502　Song: *Herbstlied.*

D503　Song: *Mailied* (unpublished).

D504　Song: *Am Grabe Anselmos* Op. 6, No. 3.

D505　Adagio in D♭ for Piano.

D506　Rondo in E for Piano.

D507　Song: *Skolie.*

D508　Song: *Lebenslied.*

D509　Song: *Leiden der Trennung.*

D510　Song: *Vedi, quanto adoro*
　　　　(from Metastasio's *Didone abbandonata*).

D511　Écossaise in E♭ for Piano.

D512　Song: *Der Leidende* called *Klage* (third version,
　　　　unpublished, other versions are D432).

D513　Quartet: *La Pastorella* for male chorus.

D514　Song: *Die abgeblühte Linde*, Op. 7, No. 1.

D515　Song: *Der Flug der Zeit*, Op. 7, No. 2.

D516　Song: *Sehnsucht*, Op. 8, No. 2.

D517　Song: *Der Schäfer und der Reiter*, Op. 13, No. 1.

D518　Song: *An den Tod.*

D519　Song: *Die Blumensprache.*

D520　Song: *Frohsinn.*

D521　Song: *Jagdlied* with chorus.

D522　Song: *Die Liebe.*

D523　Song: *Trost.*

D524   Song: *Der Alpenjäger*, Op. 13, No. 3.

D525   Song: *Wie Ulfru fischt*, Op. 21, No. 3.

D526   Song: *Fahrt zum Hades.*

D527   Song: *Schlaflied*, Op. 24, No. 2.

D528   Song: *La pastorella al prato.*

D529   Eight Écossaises for piano.

D530   Song: *An eine Quelle.*

D531   Song: *Der Tod und das Mädchen*, Op. 7, No. 3.

D532   Song: *Das Lied vom Reifen.*

D533   Song: *Täglich zu singen.*

D534   Song: *Die Nacht.*

D535   Song: *Lied* with accompaniment for small orchestra.

D536   Song: *Der Schiffer*, Op. 21, No. 2.

D537   Sonata, No. 4 in A minor, Op. posth. 164.

D538   Quartet: *Gesang der Geister über den Wassern*
        (other settings are D484, 704, 705, and D714).

D539   Song: *Am Strome*, Op. 8, No. 4.

D540   Song: *Philoktet.*

D541   Song: *Memnon*, Op. 6, No. 1.

D542   Song: *Antigone und Oedip*, Op. 6, No. 2.

D543   Song: *Auf dem See.*

D544   Song: *Ganymed*, Op. 19, No. 3.

D545   Song: *Der Jüngling und der Tod.*

D546   Song: *Trost im Liede.*

D547   Song: *An die Musik* (two versions).

D548   Song: *Orest auf Tauris.*

D549   Song: *Mahomet's Gesang.* First version, second is D721.

D550   Song: *Die Forelle*, Op. 32 (five versions).

D551   Song: *Pax vobiscum.*

D552   Song: *Hänflings Liebeswerbung*, Op. 20, No. 3.

D553   Song: *Auf der Donau*, Op. 21, No. 1.

D554   Song: *Uraniens Flucht.*

D555   A song without title or words.

D556   Overture in D for orchestra.

D557   Sonata, No. 5 in A♭ for piano.

D558   Song: *Liebhaber in allen Gestalten.*

D559   Song: *Schweizerlied.*

D560   Song: *Der Goldschmiedsgesell.*

D561   Song: *Nach einem Gewitter.*

D562   Song: *Fischerlied.*

D563   Song: *Die Einsiedelei.* Second version.
       First is D393, setting for quartet is D337.

D564   Song: *Gretchens Bitte.*

D565   Song: *Der Strom.*

D566   Sonata, No. 6 in E minor.

D567   Sonata in D♭ for Piano (first version
       of sonata in E♭, D568).

D568   Sonata, No. 8 in E♭ (for trio, see D593).

D569   Song: *Das Grab.*

D570   Scherzo in D and fragment of Allegro
       in F# minor for piano.

D571 Allegro in F# minor for piano (unfinished sonata).

D572 *Lied im Freien* for Chorus.

D573 Song: *Iphigenia*.

D573a Lesson in notation.

D574 Sonata in A for Piano and Violin, Op. posth. 162.

D575 Sonata, No. 9 in B for Piano, Op. posth. 147.

D576 Thirteen Variations on a theme by Anselm Hüttenbrenner, in A minor, for piano.

D577 *Song: Die Entzückung an Laura.* Second version, two fragments. First version is D390.

D578 Song: *Abschied* called *Abschied von einem Freunde*.

D579 Song: *Der Knabe in der Wiege (Wiegenlied)*.

D580 Polonaise in B♭ for violin and small orchestra.

D581 Trio for Strings in B♭.

D582 Song: *Augenblicke im Elysium* (lost).

D583 Song: *Gruppe aus dem Tartarus*, Op. 24, No. 1.

D583 Song: *Gruppe aus dem Tartarus* (2nd ver.).

D584 Song: *Elysium*.

D585 Song: *Atys*.

D586 Song: *Erlafsee*, Op. 8, No. 3.

D587 Song: *An den Frühling*.

D588 Song: *Der Alpenjäger*.

D589 Symphony No. 6 in C major (Little).

D590 Overture (in the Italian Style) in D for orchestra.

D591 Overture (in the Italian Style) in C for orchestra.

D592 Overture in D for piano duet.

D593 Two Scherzi, in B♭ and D♭, for piano
(arrangement of D590).

D594 Song: *Der Kampf.*

D595 Song: *Thekla.*

D596 Song: *Lied eines Kindes.*

D597 Overture in C for piano duet.

D597a Variations in A for violin solo sketches, lost.

D598 Song: *Das Dörfchen* for male chorus (sketch).

D598a Exercises (not printed).

D599 Four Polonaises for piano duet.

D600 Menuett in C# minor.

D601 String Quartet in B♭ (fragment, not printed, 32 bars).

D602 Three Marches for piano duet, Op. 27,
published as *Trois Marches héroiques.*

D603 Introduction and Variations on an original theme
in B♭ for piano duet (doubtful, see D968a).

D604 Andante in A for Piano.

D605 Fantasia in C for Piano. Fragment.

D606 March in E for Piano.

D607 *Evangelium Johannes* for soprano and figured bass.

D608 Rondo in D for piano duet.

D609 Quartet: *Lebenslust.*

D610 Trio in E for piano (to a lost minuet, probably D600).

D611 Song: *Auf der Riesenkoppe.*

D612 Adagio in E for piano.

D613 Two movements of a sonata in C for piano (fragment).

D614 Song: *An den Mond in einer Herbstnacht.*

D615 Symphony in D major. Sketches, not printed.

D616 Song: *Grablied für die Mutter.*

D617 Sonata in B♭ for piano duet, Op. 30.

D618 Deutscher Tanz with two trios and code, and two other Deutsche Tänze for piano duet.

D618a Polonaises for piano duet (sketches, not printed).

D619 Vocal exercises for two voices with figured bass.

D620 Song: *Einsamkeit.*

D621 Deutsche Trauermesse for four voices with organ (first published by Ferdinand Schubert).

D622 Song: *Der Blumenbrief.*

D623 Song: *Das Marienbild.*

D624 Eight Variations on a French Song, in E minor, for piano, Op. 10.

D625 Sonata, No. 11 in F minor for piano (incomplete).

D626 Song: *Blondel zu Marien.*

D627 Song: *Das Abendrot.*

D628 Song: *Sonett I.*

D629 Song: *Sonett II.*

D630 Song: *Sonett III.*

D631 Song: *Blanka.*

D632 Song: *Vom Mitleiden Maria.*

D633 Song: *Der Schmetterling.*

D634 Song: *Die Berge.*

D635 Quartet: *Ruhe.*

D636 Song: *Sehnsucht.*

D637 Song: *Hoffnung.*

D638 Song: *Der Jüngling am Bache.*

D639 Song: *Widerschein.*

D640 Two Ländler (unpublished).

D641 Quartet: *Das Dörfchen*, Op. 11, No. 1.

D642 Chorus: *Das Feuerwerk.*

D643 Deutscher Tanz in C# minor
and Écossaise in D♭ for piano.

D643a Quartet: *Das Grab.*

D644 Melodrama: *Die Zauberharfe.*

D645 Sketch of a Song: *Abend* (not printed).

D646 Song: *Die Gebüsche.*

D647 Singspiel: *Die Zwillingsbrüder.*

D648 Overture in E minor for orchestra.

D649 Song: *Der Wanderer* (later used as the
basis for the Wanderer Fantasy, D760).

D650 Song: *Abendbilder.*

D651 Song: *Himmelsfunken.*

D652 Song: *Das Mädchen.*

D653 Song: *Berthas Lied in der Nacht.*

D654 Song: *An die Freunde.*

D655   Allegro in C# minor for piano.

D656   Quintet for male chorus: *Sehnsucht.*

D657   Quartet: *Ruhe, schönstes Glück der Erde.*

D658   Song: *Marie.*

D659   Song: *Hymne I.*

D660   Song: *Hymne II.*

D661   Song: *Hymne III.*

D662   Song: *Hymne IV.*

D663   Song: *Der 13. Psalm.*

D664   Sonata No. 13 in A, Op. posth. 120.

D665   Quartet: *Im traulichen Kreise* (lost).

D666   Trio: *Kantate zum Geburtstag des Sängers Johann Michael Vogl.*

D667   Quintet for Piano and strings in A: *Forelle*, Op. posth. 114. *The Trout Quintet.*

D668   Overture in G minor for piano duet.

D669   Song: *Beim Winde.*

D670   Song: *Der Sternnachte.*

D671   Song: *Trost.*

D672   Song: *Nachtstück.*

D673   Song: *Die Liebende schreibt.*

D674   Song: *Prometheus.*

D675   Overture in F for piano duet.

D676   *Salve Regina (Drittes Offertorium)* in A for soprano and orchestra.

D677 Song: *Die Götter Griechenlands.*

D678 Mass No. 5 in A♭ (two versions).

D679 Two Ländler in E♭ for Piano.

D680 Two Ländler in D♭ for Piano.

D681 Eight Ländler for Piano
(of twelve, the first four are lost).

D682 Song: *Ueber allen Zauber Liebe* (unfinished).

D683 Song: *Die Wolkenbraut* (lost).

D684 Song: *Die Sterne.*

D685 Song: *Morgenlied,* Op. 4, No. 2.

D686 Song: *Frühlingsglaube,* Op. 20, No. 2
(also known as *Foi au Printemps*).

D687 Song: *Nachthymne.*

D688 Four songs: *Vier Canzonen.*

D689 Easter Cantata: *Lazarus, oder Die Feier der Auferstehung*
(fragment).

D690 Song: *Abendröte.*

D691 Song: *Die Vögel.*

D692 Song: *Der Knabe.*

D693 Song: *Der Fluss.*

D694 Song: *Der Schiffer.*

D695 Song: *Namenstagslied.*

D696 Six Antiphons for the consecration
of palms on Palm Sunday, for mixed chorus.

D697 Five Écossaises for piano.

D698 Song: *Die Fräuleins Liebeslauschen.*

D698 Song: *Liebeslauschen.*

D699 Song: *Der entsühnte Orest.*

D700 *Song: Freiwilliges Versinken.*

D701 Opera: *Sakuntala* (sketches of two acts only).

D702 Song: *Der Jüngling auf dem Hügel*, Op. 8, No. 1.

D703 Allegro in C minor for String Quartet, No. 12 (Quartettsatz).

D704 Octet: *Gesang der Geister über den Wassern* for male voices (unfinished sketch).

D705 *Gesang der Geister über den Wassern* for male voice chorus (second sketch, final version is D714).

D706 *Der 23. Psalm* for chorus with piano.

D707 Song: *Der zürnenden Diana* (two versions).

D708 Song: *Im Walde.*

D708a Symphony in D major (sketches).

D709 Quartet: *Frühlingsgesang.*

D710 Quartet: *Im Gegenwärtiigen Vergangenes.*

D711 Song: *Lob der Tränen*, Op. 13, No. 2.

D712 Song: *Die gefangenen Sänger.*

D713 Song: *Der Unglückliche* (two versions).

D714 Octet: *Gesang der Geister über den Wassern* for four tenors and four basses, with strings.

D715 Song: *Versunken.*

D716 Song: *Grenzen der Menschheit.*

D717 Song: *Suleika II*, Op. 31.

D718 Variation on a Theme by Diabelli
(see *Vaterländischer Künstlerverein*).

D719 Song: *Geheimes*, Op. 14, No. 2.

D720 Song: *Suleika I*, Op. 14, No. 1.

D721 Song: *Mahomet's Gesang*. Second version, fragment.
First version is D549.

D722 Deutscher Tanz in G♭ for piano.

D723 Aria and Duet for Ferdinand Hérold's
opera *Das Zauberglöckchen*.

D724 Quartet: *Die Nachtigall*.

D725 Duet: *Linde Lüfte wehen* for mezzo-soprano
and tenor with piano (fragment).

D726 Song: *Mignon* (first version *Heiss' mich nicht reden*).

D727 Song: *Mignon* (third version *So lasst mich scheinen*).

D728 Song: *Johanna Sebus* (fragment).

D729 Symphony in E major (sketch, not printed).

D730 Tantum ergo in B♭ for soloists, chorus, and orchestra.

D731 Song: *Der Blumen Schmerz*.

D732 Opera: *Alfonso und Estrella* (three acts, 35 numbers).

D733 Three marches militaires for piano duet, Op. 51.

D734 Sixteen Ländler and two Écossaises for piano.

D735 Galop and eight Écossaises.

D736 Song: *Ihr Grab*.

D737 Song: *An die Leier*.

D738   Song: *Im Haine.*

D739   Tantum ergo in C for chorus, orchestra, and organ.

D740   Song: for male chorus: *Frühlingsgesang*, Op. 16, No. 1.

D741   Song: *Sei mir gegrüsst!*, Op. 20, No. 1.

D742   Song: *Der Wachtelschlag.*

D743   Song: *Selige Welt*, Op. 23, No. 2.

D744   Song: *Schwanengesang*, Op. 23, No. 3.

D745   Song: *Die Rose.*

D746   Song: *Am See.*

D747   Quartet: *Geist der Liebe*, Op. 11, No. 3.

D748   *Am Geburtstage des Kaisers*
for soloists, chorus, and orchestra.

D749   Song: *An Herrn Josef von Spaun, Assessor in Linz* (Epistel).

D749   Song: *Herr Josef Spaun, Assessor in Linz.*

D750   Tantum ergo in D for chorus, orchestra, and organ.

D751   Song: *Die Liebe hat gelogen*, Op. 23, No. 1.

D752   Song: *Nachtviolen.*

D753   Song: *Heliopolis* called *Aus Heliopolis I.*

D754   Song: *Im Hochgebirge* called *Aus Heliopolis II.*

D755   Kyrie in A minor (sketch).

D756   Song: *Du liebst mich nicht* (two versions).

D757   *Gott in der Natur* for two sopranos
and two altos with piano.

D758   Song: *Todesmusik.*

D759   Symphony No. 8 in B minor (Unfinished)
(two complete movements and nine bars of a Scherzo).

D759a Overture to *Alfonso und Estrella*.

D760 Fantasia in C major, *Wanderer Fantasy*, Op. 15.

D761 Song: *Schatzgräbers Begehr*, Op. 22, No. 2.

D762 Song: *Schwestergruss*.

D763 Quartet: *Geburtstaghymne* aka *Schicksalslenker* aka *Des Tages Weihe*.

D764 Song: *Der Musensohn*.

D765 Song: *An die Entfernte*.

D766 Song: *Am Flusse*.

D767 Song: *Wilkommen und Abschied*.

D768 Song: *Wandrers Nachtlied II*.

D769 Two Deutsche Tänze for piano.

D769a Sonata in E minor for piano. Fragment, was D994.

D770 Song: *Drang in die Ferne*.

D771 Song: *Der Zwerg*.

D772 Song: *Wehmut*.

D773 Overture to *Alfonso und Estrella* arranged for piano duet.

D774 Song: *Auf dem Wasser zu singen*, Op. 72.

D775 Song: *Dass sie hier gewesen*.

D776 Song: *Du bist die Ruh*.

D777 Song: *Lachen und Weinen*.

D778 Song: *Griesengesang*.

D778b Quartet: *Ich hab in mich gesogen*. Sketch.

D779 Thirty-four Valses Sentimentales for piano.

D780 Six Moments musicaux, Op. 94, for piano.

D781 Twelve (eleven) Écossaises for piano.

D782 Écossaise in D for piano.

D783 Sixteen German Dances and two Écossaises for piano.

D784 Sonata, No. 14 in A minor, Op. posth. 143.

D785 Song: *Der zürnende Barde.*

D786 Song: *Viola.*

D787 Singspiel: *Die Verschworenen* (12 numbers), No. 3 Romanze: *Ich schleiche bang und still.*

D788 Song: *Die Mutter Erde.*

D790 Twelve Deutsche Tänze, called Ländler, for piano.

D791 Sketches for an opera *Rüdiger.* Not printed.

D792 Song: *Vergissmeinicht.*

D793 Song: *Das Geheimnis.*

D794 Song: *Der Pilgrim.*

D795 Song cycle: *Die schöne Müllerin,* which contains the following songs:

1. *Das Wandern.*

2. *Wohin?*

3. *Halt!*

4. *Danksagung an den Bach.*

5. *Am feierabend.*

6. *Der Neugierige.*

7. *Ungeduld.*

8. *Morgengruss.*

9. *Des Müllers Blumen.*

10. *Tränenregen.*

11. *Mein!*

12. *Pause.*

13. *Mit dem grünen Lautenbande.*

14. *Der Jäger.*

15. *Eifersucht und Stolz.*

16. *Die liebe Farbe.*

17. *Die böse Farbe.*

18. *Trockne Blumen.*

19. *Der Müller und der Bach.*

20. *Das Baches Wiegenlied.*

D796   Opera: *Fierabras.* In three acts, 23 numbers.

D797   Incidental music to *Rosamunde, Fürstin von Cypern,* Op. 26 (No. 3b Romanze: *Der Vollmond strahlt*).

D798   Overture to *Fierabras* arranged for piano duet.

D799   Song: *Im Abendrot.*

D800   Song: *Der Einsame.*

D801   Song: *Dithyrambe.*

D802   Introduction and variations on *Trockne Blumen,* Op. posth. 160.

D803   Octet in F for string and wind instruments, Op. posth. 166.

D804   String Quartet, No. 13 in A minor: *Rosamunde,* Op. 29.

D805   Song: *Der Sieg.*

D806   Song: *Abendstern.*

D807   Song: *Auflösung.*

D808   Song: *Gondelfahrer.*

D809   Song for male chorus: *Der Gondelfahrer*, Op. 28.

D810   String Quartet, No. 14 in D minor: *Death and the Maiden.*

D811   Salve Regina in C for quartet.

D812   Sonata in C for piano duet,
        called *Grand Duo*, Op. posth. 140.

D813   Eight Variations on an original theme
        in A♭ for piano duet.

D814   Four Ländler for piano duet.

D815   Quartet: *Gebet.*

D816   Three Écossaises for piano.

D817   Ungarische Melodie in B minor for piano.

D818   *Divertissement à la hongroise* in G minor
        for piano duet, Op. 54.

D819   Six Grand Marches and Trios for piano duet.

D820   Six Deutsche Tänze for piano.

D821   Sonata in A minor for Piano and Arpeggione.

D822   Song: *Lied eines Kriegers* for bass with unison chorus.

D823   Divertissement in E minor for piano duet
        (published as *Andantino Varié*).

D824   Six Polonaises for piano duet.

D825   Quartet for male chorus: *Wehmut.*

D825a Quartet: *Ewige Liebe.*

D825b Quartet: *Flucht.*

D826 Quartet: *Der Tanz.*

D827 Song: *Nacht und Träume.*

D828 Song: *Die junge Nonne.*

D829 Song: *Abschied.*

D830 Song: *Lied der Anne.*

D831 Song: *Gesang der Norna.*

D832 Song: *Des Sängers Habe.*

D833 Song: *Der blinde Knabe.*

D834 Song: *Im Walde.*

D835 Quartet: *Bootgesang*, Op. 52, No. 3.

D836 Chorus: *Coronach*, Op. 52, No. 4.

D837 Song: *Ellens Gesang I*, Op. 52, No. 1.

D838 Song: *Ellens Gesang II*, Op. 52, No. 2.

D839 Song: *Ellens Gesang III*, Op. 52, No. 6
      (known as *Ave Maria*).

D840 Sonata, No. 15 in C called *Reliquie*
      (third and fourth movements incomplete).

D841 Two Deutsche Tänze for piano.

D842 Song: *Totengräbers Heimweh.*

D843 Song: *Lied des gefangenen Jägers*, Op. 52, No. 7.

D844 Walzer in G called *Albumblatt.*

D845 Sonata, No. 16 in A minor, Op. 42.

D846 Song: *Normans Gesang*, Op. 52, No. 5.

D847 Quartet: *Trinklied aus dem XVI. Jahrhundert.*

D848 Chorus: *Nachtmusik*, Op. posth. 156.

D849   Symphony (known as *Gmunden-Gastein*. Watermark evidence shows this to be D944, which was wrongly dated.).

D850   Sonata, No. 17 in D, Op. 53.

D851   Song: *Das Heimweh.*

D852   Song: *Die Allmacht.*

D853   Song: *Auf der Bruck.*

D854   Song: *Fülle der Liebe.*

D855   Song: *Wiedersehn.*

D856   Song: *Abendlied für die Entfernte.*

D857   Song: *Delphine.*

D858   March for two pianos (doubtful, unpublished).

D859   *Grande Marche funèbre à l'occasion de la mort de S. M. Alexandre I, Empereur de toutes les Russies*, in C minor, piano duet.

D860   Song: *An mein Herz.*

D861   Song: *Der liebliche Stern.*

D862   Song: *Um Mitternacht.*

D863   Song: *An Gott* (lost).

D864   Song: *Das Totenhemdchen* (lost).

D865   Quartet: *Widerspruch.*

D866   *Vier Refrain-Lieder.* Individual songs are:

       Die Unterscheidung.

       Bei dir allein.

       Die Männer sind máchant!

       Irdisches Glück.

D867   Song: *Wiegenlied.*

D868   Song: *Das Echo*, Op. posth. 130.

D869   Song: *Totengräber-Weise.*

D870   Song: *Der Wanderer an den Mond.*

D871   Song: *Das Zügenglöcklein.*

D872   *Gesange zur Feier des heiligen Opfers der Messe* called
        Deutsche Messe for mixed chorus, winds, and organ.

D873   Canon a sei (unpublished).

D873a   Quartet: *Nachklänge* (sketch).

D874   Sketch of a song: *O Quell, was strömst du rasch und wild.*

D875   Quintet: *Mondenschein.*

D875a   Quartet: *Die Allmacht* (sketch).

D876   Song: *Ich bin von aller Ruh' geschieden* called
        Tiefes Leid (original title: *Im Jänner 1817*).

D877   Four songs from Goethe's
        Wilhelm Meister's Apprenticeship:

        Mignon und der Harfner (*Nur wer die Sehnsucht kennt*),
        for two voices and piano accompaniment.

        Lied der Mignon (*Heiss mich nicht reden*).

        Lied der Mignon (*So lasst mich scheinen*).

        Lied der Mignon (*Nur wer die Sehnsucht kennt*).

D878   Song: *Am Fenster.*

D879   Song: *Sehnsucht.*

D880   Song: *Im Freien.*

D881   Song: *Fischerweise* (two versions).

D882   Song: *Im Frühling.*

D883   Song: *Lebensmut.*

D884   Song: *Über Wildemann.*

D885   *Grande March héroïque composée à l'occasion du Sacre de Sa Majesté Nicolas I, Empereur des toutes les Russies,* in A minor, for piano duet.

D886   Two Marches caractéristiques in C for piano duet.

D887   String Quartet, No. 15 in G, Op. posth. 161.

D888   Song: *Trinklied.*

D889   Song: *Ständchen (Horch! Horch! die Lerch!).*

D890   Song: *Hippolits Lied.*

D891   Song: *Gesang* called *An Sylvia.*

D892   Song: *Nachthelle* for tenor solo and male chorus with piano.

D893   Quartet: *Grab und Mond.*

D894   Sonata, No. 18 in G, called *Fantasia*, Op. 78.

D895   Rondo in B minor for piano and violin, Op. 70, as *Rondeau brillant.*

D896   Sketch of a song: *Fröhliches Scheiden.*

D897   Adagio in E♭ for piano trio, called *Notturno.*

D898   Trio for Piano, No. 1 in B♭, Op. 99.

D899   Four Impromptus for piano, Op. 90.

D900   Allegretto in C minor for Piano (fragment).

D901   Quartet: *Wein und Liebe.*

D902   *Drei Gesänge*, Op. 83.

      1. *L'incanto degli occhi.*

      2. *Il traditor deluso.*

      3. *Il modo di prender moglie.*

D903   Song with chorus: *Zur guten Nacht.*

D904   Song: *Alinde.*

D905   Song: *An die Laute.*

D906   Song: *Der Vater mit dem Kind.*

D907   Song: *Romanze des Richard Löwenherz.*

D908   Variations on a Theme from Herold's *Marie* in C.

D909   Song: *Jägers Liebeslied.*

D910   *Schiffers Scheidelied.*

D911   Song cycle: *Winterreise*, which includes the following:

      1. *Gute Nacht.*

      2. *Die Wetterfahne.*

      3. *Gefror'ne Tränen.*

      4. *Erstarrung.*

      5. *Der Lindenbaum.*

      6. *Wasserflut.*

      7. *Auf dem Flusse.*

      8. *Rückblick.*

      9. *Irrlicht.*

      10. *Rast* (two versions).

      11. *Frühlingstraum.*

12. *Einsamkeit* (two versions).

13. *Die Post.*

14. *Der greise Kopf.*

15. *Die Krähe.*

16. *Letzte Hoffnung.*

17. *Im Dorfe.*

18. *Der stürmische Morgen.*

19. *Täuschung.*

20. *Der Wegweiser.*

21. *Das Wirtshaus.*

22. *Mut.*

23. *Die Nebensonnen.*

24. *Der Leiermann* (two versions).

D912 *Schlachtlied* for male double voice chorus.

D913 Quartet: *Nachtgesang im Walde.*

D914 Quartet: *Frühlingslied.*

D915 Allegretto in C minor for piano.

D916 Quartet: *Das stille Lied* (not printed).

D916a Unknown.

D916b Piano piece in C (sketch).

D916c Piano piece in C minor (sketch).

D917 *Das Lied im Grünen.*

D918 Opera: *Der Graf von Gleichen*
      (sketch, one chorus only published).

D919 Song: *Frülingslied.*

D920   *Ständchen* (*Zögernd leise*) called *Notturno* for contralto solo and chorus with piano (first version).

D921   *Ständchen* (*Zögernd leise*) called *Notturno* for contralto solo and chorus with piano (second version).

D922   Song: *Heimliches Lieben.*

D923   Song: *Eine altschottische Ballade* (two versions).

D924   Twelve Grazer Walzer for piano.

D925   Grazer Galopp for piano.

D926   Song: *Das Weinen.*

D927   Song: *Vor meiner Wiege.*

D928   Kindermarsch in G for piano duet.

D929   Trio for Piano, No. 2 in E♭, Op. 100.

D930   Comic Trio: *Der Hochzeitsbraten.*

D931   Song: *Der Wallensteiner Lanzknecht beim Trunk.*

D932   Song: *Der Kreuzzug.*

D933   Song: *Des Fischers Liebesglück.*

D934   Fantasia in C for piano and violin, Op. posth. 159.

D935   Four Impromptus for piano, Op. posth. 142.

D936   Sextet: *Kantate zur Feier der Genesung des Fräulein Irene von Kiesewetter.*

D936a Symphony in D major (Complete sketch).

D937   Song: *Lebensmut* (fragment).

D938   Song: *Der Winterabend.*

D939   Song: *Die Sterne.*

D940   Fantasia in F minor for Piano duet, Op. posth. 103.

D941   Quartet: *Hymnus an den heiligen Geist.* First version (lost), second version is D948, final version is D964.

D942   Song: *Mirjam's Siegesgesang* for soprano solo and chorus with piano.

D943   Song: *Auf dem Strom.*

D944   Symphony No. 9 in C major ('the Great').

D944A Deutscher Tanz for piano (lost).

D945   Song: *Herbst.*

D946   Three Impromptus for piano, called *Drei Klavierstücke.*

D947   Allegro in A minor for piano duet, called *Lebensstürme,* Op. posth. 144.

D948   Quartet: *Hymnus an den heiligen Geist.* Second version.

D949   Song: *Widerschein.*

D950   Mass No. 6 in E♭ for quartet, mixed chorus, and orchestra.

D951   Rondo in A for piano duet.

D952   Fugue in E minor for organ or piano duet, Op. posth. 152.

D953   The 92nd Psalm: *Lied für den Sabbath* for baritone solo and chorus.

D954   Chorus: *Glaube, Hoffnung und Liebe* with woodwinds.

D955   Song: *Glaube, Hoffnung und Liebe,* Op. 97.

D956   Quintet in C for two violins, viola and two cellos, Op. posth. 163.

D957   Song cycle: *Schwanengesang*, including following songs:

Liebesbotschaft.

Kriegers Ahnung.

Frühlingssehnsucht.

Ständchen (also called Serenade).

Aufenhalt.

In der Ferne.

Abschied.

Der Atlas.

Ihr Bild.

Das Fischermädchen.

Die Stadt.

Am Meer.

Der Doppelgänger.

D958   Sonata in C minor for piano.

D959   Sonata in A for piano.

D960   Sonata in B♭ for piano.

D961   Second Benedictus of the Mass in C, for quartet, mixed chorus, orchestra and organ for D452.

D962   Tantum Ergo in E♭, for quartet, mixed chorus and orchestra.

D963   Offertorium in B♭, for tenor, chorus, and orchestra.

D964   *Hymnus an den heiligen Geist* for eight male voices, soli, and chorus, with winds.

D965   Song: *Der Hirt auf dem Felsen* with piano and clarinet or cello, Op. posth. 129.

D965a Song: *Die Taubenpost.*

D966   Fragment of an Orchestral Score in D.

D966a Fragment of an Orchestral Score in D. (Now D71c).

D966b Orchestral sketches in A (fragment).

D967   Fugue in four parts for piano (sketch, now D37a).

D968   Allegro moderato in C and Andante in A minor,
       called *Sonatine* for piano duet.

D969   Twelve Valses Nobles for piano, Op. 77.

D970   Six Deutsche Tänze for piano.

D971   Three Deutsche Tänze for piano.

D972   Three Deutsche Tänze for piano.

D973   Three Deutsche Tänze for piano.

D974   Two Deutsche Tänze for piano.

D975   Deutsche Tanz in D for piano.

D976   Cotillon in E♭ for piano.

D977   Eight Écossaises for piano.

D978   Walzer in A♭ for piano.

D979   Walzer for piano.

D980   Two Walzer for piano.

D980a

D980b

D980c

D980d

D980e

D980f March in G for piano.

D981 Singspiel: *Der Minnesänger* (fragment, lost).

D982 Sketches of an opera.

D983 Four quartets. Op. 17.

    1. *Jünglingswonne.*

    2. *Liebe.*

    3. *Zum Rundetanz.*

    4. *Die Nacht.*

D984 Quartet: *Der Wintertag.*

D985 Quartet: *Gott im Ungewitter.*

D986 Quartet: *Gott der Weltschöpfer.*

D987 Quartet: *Osterlied* (now D168a).

D988 Canon: *Liebe säuseln die Blätter* for three voices.

D989 Song: *Die Erde* (lost).

D990 Song: *Der Graf von Habsburg* (fragment).

D991 Song: *O lasst euch froh begrüssen,*
Kinder der vergnügten Au (fragment).

D992 Part-song: *Wer wird sich nicht innig freuen* (fragment).

.

ADDENDA: D993 TO D998.

D993   Fantasia in C minor for piano. Now D2e (The second section, Andantino, is reminiscent of the corresponding section in Mozart's *Fantasia*, K475.).

D994   Allegro in E minor for piano (now D769a).

D995   Two minuets for piano (now D2d).

D996   Overture in D for orchestra (now D2a).

D997   Fragment of a Symphony in D (now D2b).

D998   Fragment of a String Quartet in (?) F.

Lightning Source UK Ltd.
Milton Keynes UK
UKHW011303060223
416544UK00001B/26